MOJANG

MINECRAFT™

THE END

MOJANG

MINECRAFT™
THE END

CATHERYNNE M. VALENTE

PENGUIN BOOKS

5 7 9 10 8 6

Del Rey
20 Vauxhall Bridge Road
London SW1V 2SA

Del Rey is part of the Penguin Random House group of companies
whose addresses can be found at global.penguinrandomhouse.com.

Penguin
Random House
UK

Published in the United Kingdom by Century, an imprint of
Penguin Random House UK, London
First published in paperback by Del Rey in 2020

Published in the United States by Del Rey,
an imprint of Random House, a division of
Penguin Random House LLC, New York.

www.penguin.co.uk

A CIP catalogue record for this book is available from the British Library.

ISBN 9781784758684

Book design by Elizabeth A. D. Eno

Printed and bound in Great Britain by Clays Ltd, Elcograf S.p.A.

Penguin Random House is committed to a sustainable future
for our business, our readers and our planet. This book is made
from Forest Stewardship Council® certified paper.

For Aurora and Cole
I am only ever a portal away

MOJANG
MINECRAFT™
THE END

Once upon a time, there was a player.

The player was you.

Sometimes it thought itself human, on the thin crust of a spinning globe of molten rock. The ball of molten rock circled a ball of blazing gas that was three hundred and thirty thousand times more massive than it. They were so far apart that light took eight minutes to cross the gap. The light was information from a star, and it could burn your skin from a hundred and fifty million kilometers away.

Sometimes the player dreamed it was a miner, on the surface of a world that was flat, and infinite. The sun was a square of white. The days were short; there was much to do; and death was a temporary inconvenience.

—Julian Gough, Minecraft "End Poem"

CHAPTER ONE

YOU AND ME AND US AND THEM

It is always night in the End. There is no sunrise. There is no sunset. There are no clocks ticking away.

But that does not mean there is no such thing as time. Or light. Ring after ring of pale yellow islands glow in the darkness, floating in the endless night. Violet trees and violet towers twist up out of the earth and into the blank sky. Trees full of fruit, towers full of rooms. White crystal rods stand like candles at the corners of the tower roofs and balconies, shining through the shadows. Sprawling, ancient, quiet cities full of these towers glitter all along the archipelago, purple and yellow like everything else in this place. Beside them float great ships with tall masts. Below them yawns a black and bottomless void.

It is a beautiful place. And it is not empty.

The islands are full of endermen, their long, slender black

limbs moving over little yellow hills and little yellow valleys. Their narrow purple-and-pink eyes flash. Their thin black arms swing to the rhythm of a soft, whispering music, plotting their plots and scheming their schemes in the tall, twisted buildings older than even the idea of a clock. They watch everything. They say nothing.

Shulkers hide in boxes nestled in ships and towers. Little yellow-green slugs hiding from outsiders. Sometimes they peek out. But they snap their boxes safely shut again, like clams in their shells. The gentle thudding sound of their cubes opening and closing is the heartbeat of the End.

And on the central and largest island, enormous obsidian towers surround a small pillar of grey stone ringed with torches. A brilliant lantern gleams from the top of each tower. A flame in a silver cage, shooting beams of light down from the towers into the grass, across a little grey courtyard, and out into the black sky.

Above it all, something slowly circles. Something huge. Something with wings. Something that never tires. Round and round it goes, and its purple eyes glow like furious fire.

Fin!

The word came zinging through the shade off the shore of one of the outer islands. A huge end city loomed over most of the land: Telos. Telos sprouted out of the island highlands like something alive. Great pagodas and pavilions everywhere. White shimmers fell from the glistening end rods. Shulkers clapped in their little boxes. Leashed to Telos like a dog floated a grand purple ship. A pirate ship without an ocean to sail. Most of the end cities had ships attached to them. No one was certain why, any more than they're certain who built all those big, strange cities in the first place. Not the endermen, though they were happy to name every place after themselves. Not the thing flying in endless circles around a gate to nowhere. Not the shulkers who never came out of hiding long enough to learn anything about anything. The end ships just *were*, as the cities just *were*, as the End just was, like clouds or diamonds or Tuesdays.

Fin! Find anything good?

A skinny young enderman teleported quickly across the island, in and out of the nooks and crannies of Telos. He blinked off in one place and back on in another until he stood on the deck of the end ship, holding something in his arms. His head was handsome, black and square. His eyes were bright and hungry. His limbs were slim but strong. An enderman leaned against the mast, waiting for him. She crossed her dark arms across her thin chest.

Naw, the enderman thought loudly. The words just appeared in the other enderman's mind. Endermen had no need for mouths or ears. No need for sound. Telepathy was so much easier than talking. You just *thought* at somebody and they understood you.

Nothing good, Mo. Just a bunch of pearls. We've got tons of those. Ugh. You take them. They give me the creeps. I was sure the chestplates we found last week would regen by now but I guess somebody else got there first. I got some redstone ore. That's about it. You go next time. You always sniff out the good stuff.

The twin twelve-year-old endermen, brother and sister, Fin and Mo, headed down into the guts of their ship. Fin was technically three minutes older, but he didn't make a big deal out of it. Things like who was older and who wasn't smacked of rankings, of structure, of Order — and Order wasn't welcome in the End.

They'd always lived here. They couldn't remember any other

place. They grew up here. It was their home. No different from any of the hundreds of endermen you'd find on any island in the archipelago. They lived on an end ship crammed with junk they'd snatched up from anywhere they could find it. Some of it was *very* good junk. Diamonds and emeralds, gold ore and lapis lazuli. Enchanted iron leggings, pickaxes of every kind, beetroot seeds and chorus fruits, saddles and horse armor (though they'd never seen a horse). Dozens of sets of marvelous grey wings you could stick right on your back and fly around anywhere you liked. Some of it was just plain old actual junk. Rocks and clay and sand and old books with broken spines. Fin and Mo didn't care. They were scavengers, and scavengers weren't picky. You never knew when you could really use some good old-fashioned clay.

The twin endermen knew there were other worlds out there. It was only logical when you lived in a place called the End. If there was an End, there had to be a Beginning. Somewhere else for this place to be the End *of*. Somewhere the opposite of here. Green and bright, with blue skies and blue water, full of sheep and pigs and bees and squid. Other endermen went there all the time. They'd heard the stories. But this was *their* world. They were safe here, with their own things and their own kind.

Fin and Mo's treasure piled up to the ceiling of the hold. The twins picked their way through their collection carefully. They'd done it a thousand times. There was a well-worn path through the boots and swords and helmets and dragon heads and ingots. Little spaces hollowed out for sitting and eating and living.

And pets.

Hiya, Grumpo, Mo thought cheerfully at the shulker in his box on the far wall. He'd always been there, just like them. They'd never been able to get rid of him, even though they really could have used his spot for more loot. If they whacked on his box until it fell apart, it just came back the next day. Eventually, they'd just given up and accepted him. Gave him a name. Let him guard the junkship some days. You never knew when someone might try to raid your ship. When you had this much loot in one place, you had to stay sharp. Grumpo didn't really *guard* it so much as just *sat there hating everything*, like he always did, but it made them feel safer. He wasn't just a shulker. He was *their* shulker.

If it was a him. They never wanted to pry. They respected the shulker's personal space.

Hiya, Grumpo thought back. He peeked out of his box. They caught a glimpse of his yellow-green head. *I hate you.*

Okay, shrugged Fin. *Good boy.*

I'm not, snapped Grumpo. *I want to bite you.*

Are so! thought Mo. *WHO'S A GOOD BOY?*

The shulker grumbled to himself and shut his box again. His last thought appeared in their heads, the letters very small and angry. *I'm a bad boy. I'll bite you tomorrow, you'll see.*

Mo and Fin dug out a basket of chorus fruits from behind a couple of blocks of ore. They divided them equally for lunch. Everything between them was equal. Very carefully, very deliberately, almost militantly equal. The twins worked quietly and happily, side by side, and packed up their meal to take with them.

Guard the ship, Grumpo, thought Fin and Mo. *We're gonna go visit ED. Don't let anyone take our stuff.*

I hate the ship, complained Grumpo, without opening his box. *I hate you. I hate ED. I hate your stuff.*

Good talk, Grumpo! They laughed inside their great black square heads.

Fin and Mo teleported out onto the deck of the end ship. The black sky looked so pretty, with the city sparkling nearby. But they weren't headed to the city. They blinked in and out of sight as they teleported across the island chain. Their ender pearls glowed hot with each jump.

In a moment or two, they'd reached the central island. Crowds of endermen moved between the obsidian towers. Beams of light from the caged lanterns shot out into the dark.

Greetings, Hubunit Paa, Fin thought to a tall elderly enderman they often saw out here. *All hail the Great Chaos!*

May the Great Chaos smile upon you, juvenile male, Paa replied solemnly. It was the traditional answer. All endermen worshipped the Great Chaos. The universe was divided into Chaos and Order. Overworlders believed in Order, but endermen knew it was a lie. Always and forever a lie. The biggest lie ever told. In the Overworld, people believed you could build a fortress strong enough to keep anything out. That you could actually make something perfect. Something that would last. Only endermen, servants of the Great Chaos, seemed to understand that this was folly. It was their holy duty to prove it. Life was so much better when you understood the truth: Anything could happen, anytime, to anyone and anything. The Great Chaos came for everyone sooner or later. It would come for the whole universe someday. The endermen's duty was to help it along any way they could. The holiest pilgrimage an enderman could make was to journey to the Overworld, witness the constructions of the Forces of Order, and sabotage them. Remove one block from a cozy house and the Great Chaos's work could begin. Rain or fire could fall through the roof. Creepers could sneak through a hole in the foundation. Thieves could crawl through and clean you out. Order was so *boring*. Wasn't life so much more interesting once you let the Chaos in?

Greetings, Hubunit Lopp, Mo thought to an enderman who was surrounded by glowing purple sparks, staring out off the edge of the island. *All hail the Great Chaos.*

Greetings, Mo, Lopp replied. *I await the return of my ender-frags. They departed to the Overworld to hunt Order and destroy it. I am tremendously proud of my fragments. They will bring glory to our End.*

I'm sure they'll be back soon, Mo thought comfortingly.

The enderman turned to stare down at them. She was so tall! Something strange flickered in her magenta eyes.

Are you alone? Are you weakened? Do you require endstack with a hubunit of superior strength and power?

Mo took a step back. Mature endermen could get very cagey about a juvenile on her own with no guardians around. It disturbed them somewhere deep in their bones. And Mo didn't like the way the big endermen thought. All stiff and formal and spiky. Long words. And too many of them. Kids didn't think like that. Fin and Mo didn't, and neither did any of the other young endermen they'd met. Some enchantment must fall on you when you came of age that turned you into a snob.

But of course, Lopp thought this way only because there were so many other endermen milling around the ender dragon's island. Alone, an enderman was angry, primitive, little better than a bear who's been hit on the head quite a lot. Only in groups did their thoughts grow all those long and interesting spikes. A group of endermen was called an End. That was why their country was called the End. All the endermen together, the biggest End there could be.

Within an End, there were many different individuals, each in a different cycle of life. Enderfrags were juveniles that fragmented off from a pair of mature hubunits. Nubunits were fully grown endermen who had not yet replicated to start their own Ends. Finally, there were cruxunits, the great, ancient ancestors that had replicated alone and started their Ends out of nothing but themselves. Coming together with other endermen to smarten up and get things done was called endstacking. Of course, it was easiest with the units and fragments of your own End. They'd known you since before you were replicated! But endermen could stack with any other endermen and grow stronger, smarter, safer, sneakier. That was what Lopp was offering: safety. One brick isn't much, though it can hurt if it falls on you. But a hundred all together are a wall.

But Mo didn't want it. She had Fin. That was enough. It had always been enough. When she stacked with endermen who were *not* Fin (and one other she was trying not to think about just now because it was just so *distracting* to think about Kan and Mo had things to do today), it made her itch all over until she wanted to claw her skin off. It made her want to cry. It filled her so full of energy she could barely keep from running and jumping and somersaulting in circles like an idiot. Mo might've been smarter endstacking, but she never *felt* smarter, because she couldn't concentrate for all the itching and crying and somersaulting. Maybe that would all go away in a few years when she became a nubunit. Mo and Fin were still enderfrags, just barely.

Or maybe Mo was just a mess. Definitely a possibility.

No, I'm fine, Mo thought fiercely.

Are you certain? thought the huge enderman with growing concern. *I am available. I am an excellent hubunit. My teleportation and fighting abilities are unequalled.*

I'm fine! Mo shouted in her head, and ran toward Fin. She did not look behind her.

And the ender dragon flew around and around and around, roaring as it went. It dipped and dove between the towers, coming to rest every so often on the small grey courtyard in the middle of the island. There, it roared some more, then took off again.

Fin and Mo teleported up to the top of one of the black pillars. They settled down on the dark stone beside the lantern and watched the ender dragon for a while. It was their favorite thing to do. No matter how long you watched ED, as they called the beast, the dragon never got any smaller or less scary or less interesting. All those nubbly scales along its spine. Those amazing wings. Those huge purple eyes. Every time it passed by they shivered with excitement and fear. But mostly excitement.

Do you ever want to go there? Mo asked, munching on her chorus fruit.

Where? Fin tracked the ender dragon with his eyes. He wasn't really listening to his twin. Who could listen to a sibling when there was a dragon around? It was resting on the little stone courtyard way down on the ground.

The Overworld.

Ugh, why? There's humans *there.*

Humans were the worst thing he knew about. Worse than the void you could so easily fall into. Worse than grown-up endermen. Worse than thieves after your loot. Way worse than Grumpo. Humans hated endermen. They *killed* endermen and stole their *hearts.* The ender pearls that every enderman was born with, the jewels that gave them the power to teleport. Who did that? Who stole *hearts?*

I dunno. Mo stretched her long, dark legs. *Meet new people. Destroy them. Get more loot. Something to eat that's not chorus fruit. Serve the Great Chaos.*

Mo, you know what happened to our hubunits. They went into the Overworld and never came back. If not for the Overworld, we would still have an End.

They got caught in the rain, Mo remembered. A horrible memory. Rain was poison to their people. Standing in a summer storm was like standing beneath a million silver bullets.

It could happen to anyone. That's what the Great Chaos teaches. It gives and it takes. It could happen to you or me or Grumpo. It could happen to Lopp's enderfrags. She stands there waiting for them every day. Have you ever seen Lopp's fragments?

No, Mo thought softly.

Fin flicked a chorus fruit over the edge of the pillar. It floated down to the yellow earth. *There you go. It does happen to anyone. How many endermen do we lose every week?*

May their noble sacrifice hasten the Reign of the Great Chaos, Mo thought piously.

Yeah, yeah, yeah. But guess who does the Forces of Order's dirty work? Humans. All our problems are because of humans. It's because of humans we can't even remember what our hubunits look like. It's because of humans we can't just pop up to the Overworld for a nice picnic whenever we feel like it. It's not worth it, anyway. I promise. Nothing up there is better than what we have here. The only good reason to visit the Overworld is to serve the Great Chaos. And I wouldn't even do that unless I was sick of being alive. What could be more Chaotic than refusing to serve anybody, after all?

Fin followed the purple spores floating around his skin with his eyes. That was how you could tell an enderman was talking, even if you couldn't hear it. The little glittering violet lights of their telepathy at work flittered all around them.

Is that what our hubunits were doing? Serving? Sacrificing?

I think so. I like to think so. That would mean us being orphans was something more than just a stupid, mean joke the Great Chaos played on us for fun.

Vengeance? Mo thought casually. *We could hunt down humans all night long. It might be fun. Steal* their *hearts for a change.*

Mo, the Overworld is dangerous. It takes people away. Why risk it?

I guess you're right. Besides, we have everything we need right here. She squeezed his dark, thin hand.

The lantern light sparkled everywhere. It was the most beautiful night the twins could imagine. Just like every night. Fin put his long, angular black arm around his twin and rubbed her square head affectionately.

Oh! she thought. *It's coming close this time!*

The ender dragon soared toward them, catching the light from each lantern it passed.

Good afternoon, ED. Mo waved shyly as the creature swooped down toward their pillar. They often tried to talk to it, though it was not tame. It rarely spoke back.

But today, something different happened.

The ender dragon turned its boxy black head toward them. It opened its great mouth. Its insides glowed violet.

Hail to thee and mercy, Mo-Fragment. Its thought blazed and crackled in her head, bigger and louder than any enderman's.

Mo froze, a chorus fruit halfway to her face. *It knows my name! How does it know my name?*

You must be famous, thought Fin. Mo felt his jealousy sizzle in her head.

The ender dragon banked and came round again. It screeched into the void.

Hark, Fragment Fin.

It knows my name too! Wow! The ender dragon turned sharply around a distant pillar. *Hark? What kind of a noise is that? Is it sick? Is it going to throw up? You got all that stuff about mercy. I got "hark."*

It means "hello," Mo giggled in the depths of her mind.

Oh! Hello, ED! Hellllooooo! Hark! Maybe it'll be friends with us! Do you think? Mo?

Mo wasn't so sure. It was coming straight for them now. The purple fire in its eyes didn't exactly look like it meant to make friends. This time, as the creature flew by, it dragged its dark wing over the top of their pillar, knocking them over like they weighed nothing at all.

NOW GO AWAY! ED bellowed in their minds. The crystal lantern next to them guttered in fear. The dragon's tail snapped in the air like a whip and it dove away into the darkness.

That. Was. Fin thought.

So. Awesome! Mo finished for him. Their purple eyes glittered with glee.

Mo grabbed a handful of the silver netting that surrounded the lantern. She could never resist a little more loot.

Race you home! she thought happily, and vanished.

Fin vanished after her.

CHAPTER TWO

THE DOME AND THE DRAGON

Fin sat on a lump of yellow hill on the very edge of Telos. He munched his chorus fruit and stared down at the courtyard below him. It forked off from the main tower of one of the smaller pagodas in the city. Above it, banners hung still in the windless night. Below it, nothing but darkness.

But inside the courtyard? Inside it was the Enderdome.

Mo didn't like to come up here. *If they don't want us, I don't want them,* she always said. Then she buried herself in something or other so she didn't have to keep talking about it. But Fin couldn't stop himself. He loved to watch the enderfrags learning, dueling, playing, sparring, drilling, even their unofficial feuds and brawls. He stayed close enough to stack with them and keep from going totally dangry (dumb and angry, Fin's own word for what endermen alone were like), but far enough away that no one could chase him off. This was where enderfrags trained to survive in the Overworld. To serve the Great Chaos. To fight humans. Fin told his twin he didn't care about the Overworld. She could see his thoughts, so it was true, or she would have called him out. But only partly true. Only mostly. Fin *didn't* care about going up to the big, bright, hot place. But he longed to train with the other fragments in the Enderdome. And the whole point of the Enderdome was to go up to the Overworld someday and punch anything you found there to pieces. He imagined himself in the Dome with the others: top of the class, popular, with ten or even *twenty* people to talk to any time he had a spare thought, instead of just his twin and a cranky shulker at the end of every day.

They were doing teleportation today. Flickering in and out of sight, up to the top of the tower and back down. Out into the hills and back to the courtyard. Here, there, and everywhere. *I could do that,* Fin thought. *I could do it so good. Better than at least half of them. Three quarters, maybe. Yeah. Definitely three quarters.*

Okay, maybe he couldn't do it that well *here*. But back home? On his ship? Fin could disappear and reappear like a deck of cards shuffling. Ace, King, Queen, Jack. Bow, stern, hold, crow's nest. No problem. But that's why he needed to be in the Enderdome with all the other enderfrags! So he could learn to do it everywhere, not just where he felt safe and comfortable. It wasn't *fair*.

Sometimes, when you teleported, it felt like you passed through other places on your way to the place you were going. As though the world got thin when you punched through it like that and you could see through to other Ends almost like this one but . . . but more peaceful, quieter, more full of everything good and useful. Fin wanted to ask about those other places, but he wasn't allowed to train, so he didn't have anyone to ask. The injustice of it burned.

But what stung, what *really* stung, was that Fin and Mo were actually pretty smart, just the two of them. Much smarter than the average enderman alone, if you asked Fin. Or Mo. They never got dangry back home on their ship, far away from anyone else. Imagine how clever they could be if they were allowed to go to the Dome with the other fragments! Endermen were always cleverest in groups, the bigger the group the better. If they were this good as a two-stack, the twins could be gods with two dozen. But they'd never get the chance.

Mo didn't think they needed training in the least. She'd even told him so that morning, as he was heading out. Well, not morning, not really. That was Overworld talk. *Order* talk. But you could make a kind of day and night out of the glow of the end rods. They got brighter and duller on a pretty regular schedule. You could think of them as a clock. If you wanted to. But that was a little bit of blasphemy. Making Order out of Chaos. Time out of timelessness. It was . . . naughty. And therefore thrilling. So, every once in a while, the twins let themselves be bad. They thought of the time when the rods shone brightest as morning, and the time when they dimmed a bit as night. But they never told anyone they'd done it.

There's nothing they can teach us that we haven't learned ourselves, Mo had thought to him that "morning." *We can build, we can hoard, we can travel, we can fight, we can think as straight and as clear as the path between the ender dragon's home and the outer islands. I like our life the way it is. I don't see why it should ever change. Just like you said before. You don't want to go to the Overworld? Well, I don't want to go to the Dome. That's how you know we're twins. We're the same, even when we're different. You don't have to go to the stupid Enderdome to learn how to sit back and have fun.*

The funny thing was, Fin knew she didn't really mean that. She didn't just like their lives the way they were. He caught her staring off into the void lots of times, dreaming of something, someone, somewhere. She would never tell him what. And he didn't pry. He could have found out if he wanted to be a jerk about it. Go peeping into the parts of Mo's mind she didn't broadcast. But that would have been rude, and he would've hated it if she'd done it to him. Fin let her have her secrets so that he could keep his. It was only fair. Fairness was a kind of Order, he knew. But secrets were seeds of Chaos, so he figured it all balanced out in the end. Either way, he knew Mo wasn't quite as happy as she pretended. A brother always knows.

Their one and only friend, an enderman named Kan, didn't understand his fixation with the Enderdome at all. *I hate training,* he always told them. *I am compelled by my hubunits to attend every day and it is boring and violent and it hurts when the other frags hit me. Taskmaster Owari never stops droning on about humans and the Great Chaos, and I spend the whole time wishing I were somewhere else, playing my music with nobody pummeling me. I even wish to be home, and I do not like home much either. When I complain, the Taskmaster only tells me that if I get stronger it will not hurt anymore. Or if I get faster they will not be able to land a blow on me. But I do not want to be strong or fast. I only want the opposite of hurt. You are so lucky you do not have to go to the Dome. Do not tell me any more about how wonderful you believe it is. You do not know. But if it will make you feel better, I can hit you several times very hard.*

But Fin didn't feel very lucky. He felt like a fragment with no hubunits, an orphan with no place in the world. He felt like a freak. Fin just wanted to be normal. He just wanted to be like the rest of them. Why couldn't he be? Why did his hubunits have to go to the Overworld in the first place? Why couldn't life just be *good*, instead of lonely, cast-off garbage? But of course, that wasn't fair. Life *was* good sometimes. And the grown-up endermen had never been cruel about it. They just . . . didn't know what to do with the twins. They were friendly enough when Fin and Mo went into Telos for supplies or to see the lights on Endermas, the great holiday when all the endermen celebrated the birth of the Great Chaos, the beauty of their land, and the strength of their family groups. Their own private Ends. Of course, the twins weren't allowed to celebrate Endermas properly. You couldn't, really, without an End. It was the one day of the year all the endermen made music, singing carols together in vast End clusters. But the twins loved to watch the lights all the same. From afar. From the outside. Like everything else in their world.

Greetings, Fin. Greetings, Mo. The adult endermen would always think when they saw them on the streets. *Are you not afraid to venture alone and weakened after the misfortune which has befallen your life?*

Thanks for bringing it up, Fin always shot back, and it usually shut them up.

It wasn't too long till Endermas now. He would have to think of something special to get Mo and Kan and Grumpo.

Suddenly, an enderfrag flashed into the grass next to him. She was small and stocky, shorter than Fin. Her black skin crackled with purple energy. The enderfrag turned to stare at him.

When you made contact with another person's thoughts for

the first time, you usually saw something welcoming. Whatever it was told you a lot about the person you were sharing minds with. Like a snapshot of their soul. When he looked into Mo's head, the image of their ship greeted him. The door to the hold was always open, and the interior always full of treasure and little beasties from all over the End. Even a tiny ender dragon perched on one of the torches. She loved animals, even though she'd never really seen any other than ED and shulkers and endermites. But she'd heard people talk about the pigs and cows and sheep and foxes and turtles and squid of the Overworld a million times, so she imagined she knew all about them. Mo's mind looked like a home full of happy animals that looked almost but somehow, at the same time, not at all like actual pigs and cows and sheep and foxes and turtles and squid. When Fin looked into Kan's thoughts, he saw musical notes dancing in beautiful spirals. Kan loved music that much. Of course, Fin couldn't see into his own head, because he lived in it. But Mo told him his was a beautiful, friendly room full of open books and pens to write in them, lying on every table and chair and the floor, too.

When he looked at this enderman's mind, Fin saw her End, all those hubunits and fragments and nubs standing close together, arms tangled around one another other until you couldn't tell where one stopped and another began.

Ugh. She was the *worst*.

By the Great Chaos, I believe I have journeyed too far and too swiftly, she gasped in his mind. *I believe you have done likewise, friend! Shall we go back together?*

Good job, Fin mumbled.

His envy burned him up inside. In a minute, she was going to flicker back to the Enderdome and he'd still be by himself with a half-eaten chorus fruit. They looked alike. But they were nothing alike. They weren't friends. They could never be friends. Even the way she thought, all those pretty, formal words. Trying to sound like grown-ups, like the big, tall endermen with their elegant telepathic speeches. Just because she was in the Dome and grown-ups liked her and probably told her she was doing a good job at being a lean, mean, human-stomping machine all the time. Well, those lovely thoughts wouldn't last. They were pretty far from the Dome now. The stack wouldn't hold. Fin had a lot of practice stacking at a distance. You had to, if you lived on the outskirts of everything. But she had no practice at all. If she stayed here more than a few minutes, just the two of them, her thoughts would be more like: *Me strong. You stupid.* And then she'd probably hit him and he'd have to decide whether it served the Great Chaos to hit her back.

Attend a moment, the enderfrag thought. Fin could feel her mind curling away from his. He knew that feeling. All the normal fragments did it when they realized who he was. One of *them.* One of the weird ones. One of the orphans. One of the Endless twins who lived out on that broken old ship like shulkers. The back of Fin's neck prickled all over. Pins and needles, like a foot that had fallen asleep. That was what it felt like when an enderman snickered nastily at you.

I do not know you, the fragment went on. Fin squirmed. *You are not in my training cluster. Why have you escaped the Dome? Where is your hubunit? Where is your End? It is lonely out here on the dunes. These are the hours of instruction. You are not allowed to be alone during those hours. No enderfrag is.*

I am, thought Fin sharply. *I am allowed, and my twin is, too.*

The fragment narrowed her magenta eyes, trying to work it out. *I don't get it.*

There it was. Her thoughts were slipping. Too much time away.

Too much time unstacked. My name is Fin. My twin is Mo. You're Koneka, right?

That is correct. Koneka shook her head. *Yeah. Koneka. But how can you know Koneka, if Koneka does not know you? Why are you out here alone and not in training with us? Alone is dangerous. Come back with Koneka.*

I have no End, Fin snapped. *I have no hubunits!* And because *I have no hubunits, the Endmoot decided I and my twin must live apart and not go to the Enderdome with you and all your happy little friends. Without an End, we could never be clever enough to deserve training. So they said.*

Oh, thought Koneka.

"Oh" is right, thought Fin. *But I can do anything you can do. You'll see. Someday. When you think about it, I and my twin are TRUE spawn of the Great Chaos. Family groups are a kind of Order, not that anyone around here notices. And I'm free of it, unlike you.*

I am gonna go now, Koneka thought sheepishly. *Dunno what do or say. So I go.*

Fine, Fin thought, and kicked the grass.

I am.

Do it then.

I go.

So go.

The enderfrag glared at him. *You stupid,* she thought nastily. Koneka vanished.

Fin stood up and walked the few short paces to the edge of the grassy island. After a moment, he pitched his fruit over the side. He wasn't hungry anymore. The young enderman watched it tumble end over end into the void. *She's stupid,* he thought. *They're all stupid. It doesn't matter.*

But it did.

Of course it did.

Mo perched on one of the high obsidian pillars on the central island of the End. She rested her back against the silver cage that held the flickering crystal flames that lit the place like little trapped moons.

The ender dragon swooped around and around. Its huge dark wings flapped up and down, up and down. Slowly, effortlessly, as though flying was ever so much easier than sitting on the ground like a lump. Its massive, blocky head moved side to side like a shark's, always seeking something, something it never found. Mo couldn't imagine what a beast like that could want. What could it lack that it could not simply take?

Every once in a while, the dragon crouched on the ground for a moment, but it was never happy there. Always, always it heaved up into the black sky again, resuming its endless circles.

No, the ender dragon's words appeared in her head like someone had written them on a vast bright piece of paper. It answered her question before she even knew she'd asked it. *I am never bored. Not in all the long, hard-boiled, seething history of existence. I ate my boredom when the comets were young. It tasted like death.*

It was happening! ED was talking to her! Her! Mo! Mo the Nobody! Way more than "hark" or "hail to thee"! And Fin wasn't even here! He was off moping at the Enderdome for no good reason. Mo didn't care one bit about the other endermen keeping their distance and making all sorts of rules about them. She cared about her twin, her loot, her friend, and her dragon.

Well, not hers, really. No dragon could ever be anybody's. But nobody was as fascinated by the great beast as Mo was. No one cared about it the way she did. As far as she could tell, no one else even bothered much with it, or was bothered by it. The ender dragon was like the sun in the Overworld. It was just *there*. It did what it did. You didn't have to try to be nice to it or have a conversation with it or love it. That would be *weird*.

ED occasionally decided the twins were worth speaking to. You never knew if today would be that day or not, though. And it was the first time it had spoken to Mo alone, without Fin. It was a very fickle dragon. And not terribly nice. But terribly *interesting* all the same. The most interesting thing in the world to Mo. She focused her thoughts and sent them across the cool air between the pillars toward the long black serpent.

All hail the Great Chaos! Mo thought joyfully.

If you must, fragment, answered the ender dragon.

Why do you keep going in the same circles on the same island all the time forever? Why don't you ever just . . . fly away? You're so big and strong, you could go anywhere. Do anything. No one could stop you. Why don't you go have adventures? That's what I would do, if I were a dragon.

ED slid one purple eye toward her as it glided lazily through the night.

Who says I am not having an adventure? Right now? Before your miserable mortal eyes?

Uh, I do. Me. You're just flying in circles. That's not an adventure. That's barely an afternoon walk.

You would think that, growled the dragon silently. *You are small. I do not expect anything else from the likes of you.*

Hey, that's not very nice. Mo was hurt, a little. She knew she shouldn't be hurt by what a monster thought of her, but she couldn't help it.

The dragon sailed higher, its thoughts falling down on her like rain. *I am not nice. So that makes a certain amount of sense, does it not? I ate nice, too, when the volcanoes had not yet learned to erupt. It was bothering me.*

Well, prove me wrong then, big guy. Tell me about your adventure.

It has not yet begun.

Then go out and get it!

You understand nothing. You are stupid and small and you understand nothing. I waste my time with you. And my time is precious beyond diamonds.

Tears sprung up in Mo's eyes. *You don't have to be so mean to me.*

I do not have to be kind, either. No law compels me. No creature can force me.

I wish I was a dragon! Then I could say whatever I wanted to anyone and they couldn't do anything back because I'd be so big and black and fearsome and I could breathe fire. And if I was a dragon I wouldn't just flap around in circles like a useless bat. She tried desperately not to cry. *I would burn down anyone who hurt me! Or hurt Fin! I would fly to the Overworld and stop every bad thing from happening! I would destroy everyone who ever hurt an enderman!* And I would bring my hubunits back, she didn't add, but felt, deeply, clutching at her heart. But that was ridiculous. Her hubunits were gone. Even a dragon couldn't get them back. She didn't even remember them, really. If you lined up all the endermen who had perished in the Overworld, Mo wouldn't even know who to save.

ED swung low, its shadow startling several elder endermen, who looked up after it with blank faces. *Child, you are not a* dragon. *You are a fragment. You are not even that. You are but a fragment of a fragment. And because you are not a dragon, it is beyond the capability of your mind to comprehend that these, right now, here, on this island, among these pillars, are the most enjoyable days of my infinite, endless life.*

I don't understand.

Yes. I said. You are stupid.

I am not!

Go away. I tire of you.

But I want to know about your adventure! Why did you talk to me if you were just going to call me names?

The best time in the world, the ender dragon hummed into her dark skull, *is the time before the adventure starts. Before it starts, it is possible, just possible, that it could end differently than it always ends. It is quiet now. Quiet is a vacation for the mind. Soon the adventure will begin, and at the end of every adventure lies pain. At the end of every adventure, you must ask if it was ever really your adventure at all. Perhaps you were only an obstacle in someone else's quest.*

Mo sighed. *I like you better when you're not talking in riddles just to make me feel dumb.*

ED let a ribbon of fire roll out of its mouth into the darkness. *I like you better when you're gone.*

Fine, Mo thought miserably. *Whatever. It's more use talking to Grumpo than you. You're nothing but nasty. I brought you lunch, not that you care. Not that I care either! It's not even for you, I just had it lying around. Whatever.*

The enderman pulled a couple of particularly ripe chorus fruits out of her pack and laid them gently on top of the pillar, where the dragon could easily reach them.

The ender dragon hovered briefly, staring at her offering.

Is it time for that already? it thought softly. *So it must be.*

I don't know what that means, Mo thought.

You are an insect to me. Insects know nothing.

I love you anyway. She always tried to tell the dragon that whenever it talked to her. So it knew, even if it ate love for breakfast and turned it into fire in its mouth.

I have no time for this. Go away. ED's tail vanished into the shadows, flying away from her.

Fine, Mo thought, and kicked the silver cage with the flame burning away within. *It's just a big dumb snake. Doesn't matter.*

But it did.

Of course it did.

Mo left the fruit where it lay and teleported away from the tall black pillar.

After a long moment, the ender dragon returned and snatched them up with its long, fiery tongue. It ate them with great relish.

MINECRAFT: THE END

CHAPTER THREE

KAN

Wake up, I hate you.

Grumpo's thoughts blinked on and off in Fin's and Mo's head like an alarm clock.

Wake up, I hate you.

Fin stretched. Endermen sleep standing up. Beds didn't really work in the End. If you made something to lie down on, it usually exploded. Endermen didn't need much sleep anyway. They were a bit like cats. They just napped wherever they were.

Wake up, I hate you. Someone is approaching the ship. I hate them. Make them leave. It's time for you to make them leave now. I hate them so much. It's happening again. Make it stop happening.

Mo grabbed one of the enchanted iron swords off the sword pile and poked her head up out of the hold. You couldn't be too careful. Humans didn't just live in the Overworld. Every once in a while one would show up here. Or so they'd been told. It hadn't actually happened yet, but sooner or later. It was inevitable. And when they saw ships practically groaning with treasure, humans tended to go a little crazy. And they started out crazy, as far as Mo was concerned.

She scanned the horizon. Telos loomed there, end rods aglow and banners flying. The night beyond was calm and deep. It always was. She didn't see anyone.

Are you sure, Grumpo? Cutie baby Grumpo.

Haaaaaate, hissed the shulker down below. *Want to bite.*

Okay, okay. Mo stuck her head out again.

Anybody there? she thought on a broad frequency that anyone should have been able to hear. *Here, human, human, human!*

I am no human, friend of mine. But I can steal your belongings if you are in the mood for humans today. The thought opened up in her mind. Mo recognized the thinker immediately. Their only friend in the End.

Hello, Kan!

Grumpo growled in his box. *See? He's happening again. I hate him. I hate how he . . . how he* happens. *It's disgusting. He comes around all the time and he does not live here and I hate him. Make him leave. Make him not happen.*

A young enderman appeared on the deck of the greyish-purple ship. He raised one long arm to say hello. In the other, he clutched a brown-checkered note block. Their friend's most prized possession. Kan was longer and thinner than Fin, but because he was always so shy, he seemed smaller than both the twins. He had big, beautiful eyes, but he was always squinting, trying to hide them, trying to make them unnoticeable.

Because Kan's eyes weren't like the wide, clear magenta-violet eyes of other endermen.

Kan's eyes were green.

No one knew why. No one could remember any other enderman who had green eyes, not in all the history of the End. It bothered people. Sometimes it bothered them a lot. Nobody in Telos looked Kan in the eye if they could help it. Fin and Mo had never minded. Some people are just born different, that was all. Some people were orphans. Some people had green eyes. Mo thought they were amazing. Nothing else in the End was exactly that color. Kan's eyes were green like the grass in the Overworld. Green like emeralds. Green like the leaves of a tree in the sun.

Kan raised his dark hands to greet her.

I have run away again, the green-eyed enderman announced triumphantly. *My hubunits attempted to retrieve me, but they could not. I am faster. Taskmaster Owari attempted to drag me back, but she could not. I am stronger. So their training has worked, but not as they hoped. They are all the worst. Every time I think I can bear it, they prove me wrong. May I hide here with you?*

You're always welcome, Mo thought. *Come in, come in!*

That is the opposite of what I said! wailed Grumpo.

And there was the gang. They'd always been like this: Fin and Mo and Kan, morning, noon, and night. Inseparable. The best of friends. Not that Kan's hubunits approved much of that. Not that anyone approved much of that.

Fin and Mo lived on the outskirts of Telos. They lived on the outskirts of everything. They had no End. To everyone else, all these things made them dangerous. To Kan, it made them exciting. Your End was everything. So Fin and Mo should have been nothing. But they weren't nothing. They weren't nothing, at all. What made an enderman an enderman was the End they belonged to, the End that belonged to them. And that was why no one in Telos seemed to know what to do about Fin and Mo, living off on their own in a ramshackle old ship after their hubunits failed to return from the Overworld. Most people thought them frightfully stupid. How could they be anything else when their End consisted of nothing more than two endermen and a shulker? That wasn't an End. That was just . . . a load of junk. So mostly, *mostly*, the other endermen left the twins alone. They had trouble only when they tried to go into the city.

But Kan knew a secret about the twins. They weren't stupid at all. They were much better company than the enderfrags at the Enderdome or the awful Taskmaster or any of the hubs and nubs and fragments Kan had ever met. Maybe it was a twin thing. Kan didn't know any other twins. Maybe they were all like that. Maybe it was like his green eyes. Just some freak of nature. But somehow, just the two of them were enough. Even though a two-stack was usually just barely enough to count to ten between them. Three were the minimum for a decent conversation. Except that Fin and Mo stacked, without any help from anyone. And all three of them were positively *plenty*.

Kan was part of an End, all right. Just like all the other enderfrags. But they never seemed to be much a part of him. He was forever running away from home. This was the third time that week. Kan hated the way he felt when he ran away. He hated the way he felt all the way up until he got to the ship. Mean and dumb and angry and hurt, barely able to remember where he was running to or why. But all he had to do was step on board the ship and the cool cascade of endstacking started up. He could feel himself getting beautifully calm and clever. Because he was home. Not with his End, but with his friends.

Mo had never met any other enderman who'd run away from home even once. But Kan did it every three or four days. Not that

Mo judged her thin, dark friend. She understood, at least she thought she did. Mo would have hated it if she was stuck in some sour, crappy club full of people who scowled at her all the time and told her what to do. Who to be. She would have run away too. And she didn't think anyone should be punished for running away. It was all part of the Great Chaos. Staying somewhere you hated because the rules said you had to was giving in to the Forces of Order.

Mo led her friend down into the hold. Fin was frying chorus fruits in an iron chestplate over the torch flames. You could make a weird kind of sour purple popcorn that way. They'd never found a way to eat it safely, but it was pretty fun to watch the kernels pop. Every once in a while, Grumpo would eat a handful if you sprinkled it into his box like fish food. *Thanks*, he'd say. *I hate it. I want to bite you.* But he always ate it all up anyway. And refused to tell them how he managed to digest the stuff.

Fin waved one long black hand at them, stuck inside the enchanted iron gauntlet that they used as a cooking mitt. The fruits popped cheerfully—Pop! Pop! CRACK!

Kan inhaled the aroma of the chorus corn deeply. It smelled horrific. But it smelled like home.

I like your house so much better than mine, he thought sadly. *I wish I could live here with you.*

No room, Fin thought back jokingly. But the thought that he did not allow to float between their minds was: That would be great, but your hubunits would literally, actually kill us. They'd sweep through this ship like a shadow made of knives and we'd never make gross, inedible popcorn again.

Kan settled into a corner of the ship's guts, between a block of emerald and a pair of old boots. He put his note block between his legs. For a while, he just lay his head on top of it. He didn't think anything. At least not out loud. Endermen could hide their thoughts if they really wanted to. It was just considered incredibly, aggressively rude. Kan didn't cry. Endermen couldn't, not really. But in their minds, Fin and Mo could see an image of the little white sparkles that fell from the end rods on the tips of the towers of Telos, falling all the way to the ground. They understood what that meant the same way any human knows what water falling from another human's eyes means.

Finally, Kan began to tap the brown thatch of his note block. Fin sighed eagerly and sat down with his long legs crossed. Mo leaned forward to hear better. *No one* could play a note block like Kan. Sure, the twins found them every now and again. Mostly when a human failed to kill the ender dragon (as they always did) and dropped one when they got what was coming to them. But when Fin or Mo tried to play it, all they got were short, sharp sounds that they could never fit together into a song.

When Kan played, even the sky stopped to listen.

His hands moved over the top of the block and music poured out. It filled the ship's hold and spilled out onto the deck. The song was sad and bright and angry and hopeful all at the same time. But it was quick and light, too. You couldn't help but tap your feet to it. It made you want to dance and it made you want to hug your friends and it made you want to run out and conquer the world, or at least conquer anyone who tried to tell you what to do.

Grumpo's box top rose up slightly. His yellow-green nub of a head peeked through the crack. Kan stopped playing.

Let me guess, he thought at the shulker, *you hate it*.

After a long pause, the shulker answered: *I don't hate it.*

A gasp rose from all three of the endermen. They couldn't believe it. Of course Kan was good. The best. But Grumpo hated *everything*. Kan often thought the shulker was like his hubunits that way.

I just *STRONGLY DISLIKE IT*, the shulker snapped back, and slammed his box shut.

Kan turned his friendly rectangular head back to his friends. He had always been the handsomest enderman in the End. Mo thought so. Fin thought so. But whenever the three of them went to Telos and passed others on the long violet streets, they always heard the grown-ups thinking about how ugly and awkward Kan was. How horrible his eyes were. How stupid and weird and even hideous he was. It made Mo so angry. Kan was beautiful! Why couldn't they see it? If only the whole of Telos could hear him play . . . but hearing him play never seemed to help Kan's family like him any better.

I was playing that song this morning. My secondary hubunit heard me. He was so furious. He is right. He has told me time and time again to give up my block. Stop it, *he screamed,* stop that horrible racket! Music is one of the chief servants of Order! How dare you bring it into this house! I cannot stand one more note! Be who you were meant to be! Be one of us! Go to the Overworld! Hunt humans! Serve Chaos like your fellow enderfrags! Eat, fight, and be merry! Why must you mope and sing all the time? You are not a sad parrot! *And then he tried to break my block.*

I'm sorry, thought Fin. *I wonder if our hubunits would have been like that.*

But then, if I try to get away, if I try to save my block, it only gets worse! Without me, my primary and secondary hubunits, their hubunits and nubunits, their other enderfrags and all the rest of them are weaker and dimmer. They roar and chase after me and try to get me back into their End even though I do not want to be in their End at all! I do not want to go to the Overworld! I do not care one bit about the Overworld! It's bright and horrible there! I do not want to be a warrior. I do not care about the Great Chaos!

Mo gasped. That was blasphemy. Real, serious blasphemy. If a grown-up heard them thinking like that . . .

I do not want to be an enderman at all if all it means is hunting humans and fighting battles and breaking things. I just want to play my music. I like this familial group! Kan and Fin and Mo and Grumpo and the ship! That is my End. They do not understand me. They will NEVER understand me.

We like this End, too, thought Fin.

They were all quiet for a while.

How long before they come to get you? Mo thought delicately. Kan wouldn't want to talk about it, but whenever his hubunits came to pick him up, they tended to do quite a bit of damage to the ship.

I do not know. Kan's thoughts were so quiet they were like whispers. *I wish I did not have hubunits.*

Don't say that, Fin thought fiercely.

No, you don't, thought Mo at the same time.

Now Kan's thoughts were so quiet they could barely see them. They flickered in the twins' heads like candles about to go out. *Then I only wish I had not been born different. I wish I liked to fight and break things like everyone else. I wish I had never heard music in the first place. I just want to be normal. Why did the Great Chaos make me this way?*

I think you're wonderful this way, Mo thought.

Grumpo's box clapped open suddenly. Then shut again. Then

open. Then shut and open and shut and open and shut again, but faster and louder. *SOMEONE IS APPROACHING THE SHIP,* the shulker screeched into their skulls. *SOMEONE IS APPROACHING THE SHIP. SOMEONE BIG. HATE. HATE. HATE. HATE. I WILL BITE THEM. I WILL. LET ME BITE THEM. YOU WILL NOT BE SORRY. EVERYTHING WILL BE BETTER IF I BITE THEM. TRUST GRUMPO. GOOD BOY GRUMPO.*

Fin and Mo turned toward the door into the hold. The terrible thoughts of Kan's secondary hubunit, Karshen, appeared in their minds like flashing lights and sirens.

KAN! WHERE ARE YOU LOCATED IN THE VOID?!

Full of rage. Full of pride. Full of that strange way of talking grown-ups liked so much. There were enough of them here that Karshen could summon the intelligence to speak as he pleased.

KAN! I WILL DISCOVER YOU!

I will go, Kan thought glumly. He tucked his note block under his skinny, dark arm. *I do not want any of your treasure to get ruined like last time. The behavior of my hubunits humiliates me. I am sorry.*

KAN! YOU ARE MORE FOOLISH THAN YOU APPEAR! UNCOVER YOURSELF TO YOUR HUBUNIT! WE DO NOT POSSESS AN EXCESS OF TIME IN WHICH TO PLAY YOUR FRIVOLOUS GAMES. UNCOVER YOURSELF. EVENTS COMMENCE. TERRIBLE EVENTS.

One enderman alone may not be as clever or as strong as many endermen together. But one enderman alone is still plenty strong. They could hear him thrashing around on the upper deck. They heard the slats of the ladder on one side of the mast crack under his fist.

I will go, Kan said again. But he didn't get up.

What's he talking about? Mo thought swiftly. *What terrible events?*

I do not know, nothing was afoot when I left. All was silence. Except for the usual yelling session concerning how much all sensible people hate music.

KAN!

It is the day of my fragmentation, Kan thought glumly. *They do not even remember.*

Endermen were not born the way humans were. The little enderfrags just replicated off the primary hubunit. A tiny black sprite blinking away from a big black block. They looked almost like small black eggs. No pain or drama or cuddles in its mother's arms. A newborn enderman was just part of the primary hubunit one moment, and off on its own the next. But they did celebrate their day of fragmentation, all the same. Usually.

Now they could hear the thoughts of Kan's primary hubunit, Teg. Even louder than Karshen's. Her heavy feet crunched onto the ship.

They're going to wreck the place, Fin worried.

KAN YOU MUST REVEAL YOURSELF TO YOUR CREATORS!

Farewell my friends, waved Kan as he trudged up the steps toward his family. *I will see you again. Someday. I hope.*

It'll be okay, Mo thought after him.

Will it, though?

Ender swear, Fin assured him.

Ender swear, Mo agreed.

Kan nodded. His face looked so pretty in the soft light of the End. *Okay. I believe you.*

KAN, YOU HAVE APPEARED AS IF BY MAGIC. The huge endermen outside blared their thoughts everywhere with very little care for who heard them. They must really have been worried. Usually, endermen were much more careful to keep their thoughts tight and directed, like a flashlight's beam that landed only where you wanted it to.

How did you find me so swiftly? Kan thought dryly.

You always come here, Kan's primary hubunit thought, returning to a normal volume. *Why would we look in an alternative location?*

But his secondary hubunit was still screaming at the top of his mind.

YOU MUST RETURN TO THE HOME NODE IMMEDIATELY, FRAGMENT. THERE IS NO TIME TO EXPEND IN DISCUSSING YOUR FAILURES.

Why? What is at home? More yelling? Kan's thoughts were white-hot with resentment.

The primary hubunit crouched on her black knees. The lights of Telos beyond her enormous head gave her a strange yellowish halo. She looked deep into her fragment's strange, terrible green eyes. She even touched his head. Just a little. Almost as if she cared. And now, even though Fin and Mo and even Grumpo could still hear her thoughts, she sent her words quietly.

Kan, fragment of mine, you must come home and prepare. It is imperative. We must defend ourselves. The humans are coming.

CHAPTER FOUR

THE ENDMOOT

Humans.

Even the word made Mo shudder.

Humans.

Fin had never seen one, and he didn't want to.

Oh, they came to the End. Every once in a while. Like pests. Like Creepers sneaking up behind you on a sunny day. Silverfish leaping out at you from a path you thought was safe. Spiders turning on you just as the sun sets. Or worse, endermites chewing at the foundation of the world until it cracked.

But to Mo and Fin, all that was just stories. Rumors. Memories. Other people's memories. Just as they had been told by the elders what their hubunits were like, they had been told what humans were like. Just in case. In case they needed to know, someday. To protect themselves.

Humans were strange. They were alien. They were hideous. Instead of beautiful, sleek black bodies as tall as trees, they were short and thick and a hundred different colors all mushed together into fat eyes, wet stomachs, horrible reeking feet, and something particularly nasty called "hair." They were violent and angry even when they had everything they could want. If you put a human in a nice patch of swamp or forest or meadow, they'd carve out everything valuable for themselves in half a day, if that. They just sucked it up like squishy flesh tornadoes. And all to build a stupid house or castle or statue, instead of leaving it as it was, unspoiled, which had been far more beautiful than their weird ugly buildings in the first place. Sometimes, they just hit sheep and pigs and even rocks with swords for *fun*. Just to see what would happen. As if they didn't know. And if they saw you, if they so much as *saw* you, they'd get you. You *had* to get them first. That was all there was to it. Survival of the quickest. Once you've seen one human, it's too late. They'll be everywhere before you can blink.

You could get them easier at night. They had to sleep on beds, in houses. Endermen catnapped with their eyes slitted, just slightly open, ready and wary of predators. Obviously, the sensible way to get your rest! One of the elders, a lanky, gruff old one named Sama, had had to explain to the twins that for humans, "sleep" meant lying in one place for hours and hours, totally unable to hear or see anything. This seemed idiotically dangerous, and they told Sama so. The elder had agreed, and they'd gone their separate ways, satisfied to be right all around. That was why humans needed beds and houses, to keep them safe while they did their idiot thing at night. So the best bet was to catch them before they could get into their little fortresses.

And of course, as Fin and Mo knew very well, humans' favorite thing to eat was hubunits.

Not that they'd ever asked anyone what humans' favorite food was. They didn't need to. It was quite literally the story of their lives.

Humans were monsters. Storybook horrors.

And they were coming.

An Endmoot had been called.

Because endermen were most intelligent and careful in their family groups, the wisest an enderman could possibly be was at an Endmoot. From all over the End, endermen came in their family groups to the ender dragon's island to commune and plan. Whenever a decision that affected all of them had to be made, they came to stand in the long shadows of the obsidian pillars and become wise together. It was not every enderman who existed. That was impossible. Endermen ranged far and wide, in every part of the world. It wasn't even every enderman in the End. The End was so vast, each section of it could go eons without communication with another section. But it was enough. Enough to choose the right path.

As long as Fin and Mo had been alive, there had been only one Endmoot: when their hubunits died and no one knew what was to be done with the orphans. There'd never been a need for another. The End had stayed peaceful all that time. A raid here or there from overworlders, sure. But nothing that required a plan of action to handle.

Until now.

They came drifting in like black birds, in groups of four and five, six and eight, sometimes even twelve and fifteen or more. Their lovely broad heads tipped up toward the crystal light falling from the towers, toward the shadows of the eternally circling dragon, who played no part in these affairs and offered no advice. Sparkling violet dust glittered all around the endermen as they gathered. There was Sama, the elder who had explained sleep to them once upon a time. There was Lopp, whose enderfrags had still not returned. There was Paa, who had long ago brought them the news that they could not train at the Enderdome now that there were only two of them. There was Eresha, the Mouth of the Great Chaos, with her many clerics gathered around her. There was Kraj and Karshen and Teg and Wakas and the beautiful nubunit Tapi. Fin even saw Koneka hiding behind her hubunits, awed by so many people in one place. Kan was there too, sulking on a low dune with his note block beside him. His strange green eyes stared off into the distance. Kan kicked at the sand and grass with his feet. The twins saw everyone they knew. Many, many more they did not.

ALL HAIL THE GREAT CHAOS! Eresha thought over the crowd, the power of her mind as commanding as a trumpet.

MAY THE GREAT CHAOS SMILE UPON YOU, answered the masses of endermen.

How do we know humans are coming? Mo thought to her twin. A quick, direct thought between the two of them, not to be shared with anyone else. *Are there . . . I don't know, alarms? Human alarms?*

Can you not feel it? The thoughts of an elder came slicing into their conversation. Rude. But all rules and niceties were off now. The danger was too great for manners. Owari, the Taskmaster of the Enderdome, towered above them. *The twelve seals are nearly in place. And upon those seals the humans will place twelve eyes of ender. When it is done, the great portal shall be complete, and they will swarm into our world. It is the End Times.*

Twelve eyes? Fin recoiled in horror. *EYES? What is wrong with them? Whose eyes did they steal? For what? Party decorations?*

Humans do worse than that, juvenile male, thought Karshen, Kan's secondary hubunit. He was calm and thoughtful now, stacked with so many endermen. Not a trace of his rage left. *They steal our pearls.*

Mo felt sick. Ender pearls were to an enderman as a heart and a soul were to a human. *Why? By the Great Chaos, why?*

Karshen answered: *With it, they can teleport as we do.*

They can't walk? Mo thought in horror. *Run?*

They walk very well indeed, and run better than most. But with an ender pearl, they arrive at their destination somewhat faster.

And that, to a human, was apparently worth ripping the soul from an enderman. They wouldn't even know who it had belonged to. An enderman's entire heart was nothing more than a minecart ride.

It only works once for them, Kan thought from his sullen perch on the edge of the island. Distance mattered little when it came to telepathy. If you wanted to be heard, you could be. His purple spores sparkled brightly. *The pearl burns out into an ember of coal after they use it.*

Oh, that's fine then! Fin cried. *Very efficient! We're just like torches to them! Burn us and throw us away.*

I hate them, Mo thought. *I hate humans so much.*

A howl of rage went up from the minds of hundreds of endermen. White-hot, black-cold, insatiable fury.

The moment I see one I cannot stop myself, hissed Nubunit

Tapi, shaking with anger. *I cannot rest until I kill it. My soul burns until it is dead.*

Good, my friend! Thought an extremely tall enderman standing nearby. *That is right and proper! Let your lust for battle guide you! Strike them all down in the name of the Great Chaos! Break their castles! Take their treasure! Feel no guilt. They would do the same to you.*

It is true that humans are the greatest scourge the world has ever known, as disgusting as endermites, as greedy and ugly as death itself. That thought belonged to the elder Ipari. It floated in the minds of all the gathered endermen, cool and firm. *But we have little time for this. Each and every enderman must feel the portal nearing completion, like locks sliding into place within us.*

The smallest enderfrags looked around themselves suddenly, terrified, expecting a human to appear at any moment.

Ah, the little ones do not understand as their hubunits do, the elder Ipari thought soothingly. *Time in the Overworld does not flow in precisely the same way as it does here. In the time it takes for whatever humans are building their portal to slide another stone, another eye into place, hours or days may pass in the End. We cannot know for certain. Time is the servant of Order. We are not friendly with it.*

I don't feel anything, Fin thought quietly. *Do you?*

No, answered Mo. *Maybe we're getting sick. Grumpo had that cold, remember? He told us to snuggle up close so we would get it, too.*

But we do know the time is short, another enderman, Beigas, picked up Ipari's thought where it left off. His violet eyes flashed. *The portal will open beneath the very earth on which we now stand. And they will pour out like lava. We must fight them. That much is certain. Perhaps we can trust in our dragon to protect us?*

The endernation looked to the skies.

No answer came but a long, low reptilian laugh.

A single word echoed in all their minds: *Fools.*

The End belongs to us, thought Wakas, one of the endermen shepherds. She had a flock of shulkers she tended on the slopes of one of the smaller inner islands. *It is the land of our people. We have lived here since the beginning. They have no right to take our country from us and pillage it.*

Not exactly since the beginning, Vegg interrupted her. Vegg was a strategy master in Telos. She taught the class Fin had watched yesterday from his dunes. Fin watched her now, longingly. She was giving a lecture, a real lecture. And he was here to listen. Finally.

You speak nonsense, Vegg. Be silent, snapped Wakas.

Nonsense? Did we build these cities? Did we raise these towers, block by block? Did we plant the chorus trees? Did we light the crystal torches atop those pillars? No. We did not. Our ancestors found them as they are. Someone was here before us, and we took their land just as the humans wish to take ours. We took it so thoroughly that now we do not even remember their names or what they looked like. And besides, ownership is Order.

I would not go that far, began Eresha, the Mouth of the Great Chaos. *The human invaders believe everything is theirs for the taking. That is the Order of the universe in their twisted minds. They see a thing they desire; they smash it. They take it. They devour it. They destroy it. They use it in their vile constructions. We must stand against that. We must keep the End safe and whole, and though there is some Orderliness to our possession of this place, it is outweighed by our needs. Endermen must rule the End. The Great Chaos wills it so.*

There is another dilemma, an enderman named Kraj piped up.

A great silence fell in all their minds. Kraj was the oldest ender-man any of them had ever heard of. He was a cruxunit. One of the thick, powerful stems from which all other endermen sprang. The violet of his eyes was faded, his spores almost silver. *I am more ancient than many of you. I have seen more things. Suffered more. Experienced more. I have escaped the rain all the days of my life.*

Get on with it, Kraj, Paa complained. *You impress no one.*

Fin and Mo were stunned. They had always been told to re-spect the cruxunits. But Kraj really didn't impress any of the other elders. As soon as his thoughts fired up, the other endermen started looking bored and restless. They picked at their spores, wandered around, examined the wall of a nearby pillar with sud-den intense interest. No one listened to Kraj, and most seemed to intensely wish he'd stop talking at once. The twins took the op-portunity to jog over to Kan and settle down on the dry grass with him. The night sky loomed over the edge of the island. It was so beautiful. They'd always thought so.

Kraj kept talking, pointedly ignoring the endermen pointedly ignoring him. The ways of adults were very strange. *I have jour-neyed to the Overworld many, many times. I have always returned. I have been attacked by humans, cut and beaten. I have barely avoided being caught in the rain. I have served the Great Chaos in the Overworld and the End. And I must warn you that humans have discovered a terrible secret to use against us. For centuries, they could not hide from the ender gaze. Once we saw them, they were ours. But in the Overworld there grows a certain squash, a certain gourd, a pumpkin round and thick. If you had not jour-neyed as far and as long as I, perhaps you might not have noticed it. Bushes here and there, vines that looked black and welcoming, like endermen, somehow. Friendly. Kind. The humans discovered this. They hollow out these pumpkins and wear them like helmets. When they hoist the gourd-helm over their cursed skulls, we cannot tell the difference between them and an enderman. They can walk among us, spies, secret operatives, double agents! Even now, the humans could already be among us, and we would suspect nothing!*

A terrible shriek of despair echoed around the ender dragon's island. And then, like thunder after lightning, the long, low laughter of the dragon followed.

Is there anything we can do against such a weapon? wailed Lopp.

Is there any way to know which of us are truly endermen? thought Karshen, staring intensely toward the edge of the island. Toward Kan and that blasted note block.

There is not, admitted Kraj. They were listening now, weren't they? Oh, yes. Now they paid attention. Kraj reveled in it. *We must be careful. Never travel alone. Move in groups of four at least, and more if you can gather them. We have never needed one another so much. Fortify yourselves. Have faith in the Great Chaos. It will guide and protect us. It will visit ruin upon our enemies. Place shulkers everywhere you can. They are coming, if they are not already here. We must be ready. We must protect our land from the interlopers.*

Tapi frowned, but kept her thoughts to herself.

But there must be a way to tell, thought Karshen. His eyes narrowed into magenta slits in his black head.

Is he looking at us? Fin thought, terrified.

He's looking at us, Mo thought back. *I wish we hadn't come. He's crazy.*

Karshen glared at them. *Through* them. *It is impossible that the humans have invented something so effective that no enderman can see through their deception. Humans may be strong, but they are wicked and stupid. They use their mouths to talk, like animals. The same mouths they eat with. No one who talks with their eating hole can best the noble enderman. There must be clues that would reveal the spies! If you look closely enough.*

I did not say there were *spies,* thought Kraj hurriedly. *Only that there* may *be. Do not rush to suspicion. The true servant of Chaos accepts all possibilities.*

But Karshen ignored the cruxunit. *A* clue, the hulking hubunit growled in their heads. *If only someone was wise enough to see it. They would not be like us. Oh no. They would be different. Freaks. Outcasts. Monsters. People who simply* cannot *act normal, no matter how you try to accept them. People with no respect, no manners, no love for the End. People who reject the endergroup altogether and run off to be . . . to be . . . by themselves. UGH! Humans could never understand the meaning of family. They are the same alone or together: ugly, dumb, unpleasant, annoying, and cruel.* Karshen had worked himself into a fury. His slick, dark shoulders quivered and began to burn red. The berserker rage of the enderman who has a human in his sights. *And LOUD,* he finished.

Stay away! Mo yelled. *You don't know us! You don't know anything about us!*

Please, Karshen! Fin scrambled up. A few blades of grass and grains of sand skittered off the edge of the island, tumbling into the void. *We've eaten with you and drunk with you! You took us in when our hubunits got caught in the rain! You do know us! You've known us since we were little! We don't even know what pumpkins are!*

Karshen bellowed the enderman war cry and bolted toward them, screaming, shrieking. The sound was like a horrible mechanical siren.

KAN! the hubunit roared. He swung his long arms, knocking Mo and Fin aside like black dolls. He kicked the note block off the ender dragon's island into the night with a yelp of joy and triumph. Kan cried out after it, white tears streaming in his mind. It fell silently, slowly, until it disappeared into the dark. Karshen grabbed his fragment's head and smashed it against the earth as though he meant to crack it open. Surely no pumpkin could withstand more than a few blows like that. *I knew it! I knew it all along! Everything makes sense now. You are not my fragment! You have never been my fragment! You are a HUMAN BEING WITH GREEN EYES!*

Kan gave up. He lay on the ground beneath his hubunit and cried.

CHAPTER FIVE

THE SPY

Fin and Mo carried Kan back to their ship. They each put a shoulder up under one of his slender arms and flashed through the island chain with a couple of easy teleports they barely felt. They didn't want to jostle him too much. It was quiet on their ship. The roar of the Endmoot lay far behind them. Only the flicker of end rods and the slow thudding of Grumpo's box like a heartbeat deep within the end ship welcomed them home.

Is your head okay? Mo whispered.

Kan moaned. They heard it only in their minds, but a moan in the mind is much worse than one you hear with your ears. You can't try to moan less loudly so your friends don't worry about you when they can hear the inside of your head. You can't hide anything.

Sit here, Fin thought. *I'll get something to clean you up. I'm pretty sure I've got a potion of healing around here somewhere.*

Why are you helping me? Kan thought bitterly. *You heard him. I am a filthy, disgusting, ugly, loud human. Stop helping. You do not help a spy once you have caught him. You interrogate him. I am ready.*

Grumpo's box thudded several times. They heard muffled laughter.

Listen when Grumpo hates something, the shulker chuckled. *Told you. Told you. No one listens to Grumpo's hates. Grumpo has the best hates. He hates for good reasons. Ha, ha, Kan, I hate your face. I want to bite your face so hard. Do you want to know a secret? If you let Grumpo bite who he pleases, life will be so much better for everyone.*

Shut up, snapped Fin. *Not now, Grumpo.*

You can bite me, Grumpo, Kan thought miserably. *I deserve worse than the bite of a shulker.*

Oh, Kan. Hush. Mo rummaged behind one of the barrels in the hold for a minute. When she emerged, she was holding something in her hand. She gave it to Kan. *Eat this. You'll feel better.*

It was a golden apple. Mo had only two. They were terribly precious. She'd found them in the back alleys of Telos, on top of a pile of dust that she assumed had once been a human. Caught thieving by a righteous enderman, no doubt. They'd probably been trying to heal themselves by eating the apple when the good citizen rushed them. Served whoever it was right. Mo had laughed at the dust. *You died,* she'd thought. *Dummy. Only dummies die.*

Kan ate the apple slowly. His jaw obviously hurt. But slowly, the purple blood dried up and flaked away. The bruise on the side of his head faded and vanished. The enderman sat up straight again.

He didn't look any different. He was as black and beautiful as ever, the angles of his face sharp and clean. His eyes were the same bright, glittering green they were so fond of. There was no sign of pumpkin anywhere. Not one bit of seed or stringy pulp.

Karshen's wrong, thought Mo. *Of course he's wrong. How could you think for a minute you didn't belong here? You're an enderman, just like us. You've always been an enderman. Your hubunit is just . . .*

An idiot, Fin finished his sister's thought. *And a bully.*

But if I was human you would not be able to see it! Kan protested. *I would look normal to you! I am human. I am. It explains everything. My music. My . . . my eyes. It is the only thing that makes sense.* The enderman sniffled and wiped his eyes as though he wished he could wipe them away completely. *Humans love music, you know. Oh . . .* he remembered suddenly. *My note block. It is gone . . . gone.*

A memory flashed between them: Kan finding that note block on one of the inner islands years ago. Little Kan with his little shining green eyes, wandering alone on a little scrap of land floating in space with one measly tree on it. Alone because he couldn't stand his house anymore. Because his fellow-fragments had called him *greenboy* again that morning and he hated himself. Hated that he'd cried. Hated that they hated him. Hated his eyes for their greenness. Wishing every day he'd wake up and they'd be pink. And then he saw it, lying on the yellowish earth next to a pair of boots, a broken sword, and a packet of apples and cooked cod, like destiny waiting for its person. He hadn't even known what it was at first. He'd just touched it. Innocent as anything.

But when Kan touched that silly brown block, it sang.

And now it was gone.

Kan, no pumpkin in the world could survive what your hubunit did to you, Mo thought.

You do not know that. Do you even know what a pumpkin is?

Well, not exactly. Almost. Kraj said it was a gourd. I suppose that is some kind of fruit?

See?

Fin shook his friend by the shoulders. *Kan! How could you POSSIBLY be a human? Remember that Endermas when we were all five? Your hubunits let us come to your settlement and share the Enderfeast of Divine Chaos. It was the only year they let us past the home perimeter. Do you remember?*

Yes, Kan mumbled.

Do you remember why they let us?

Because I begged. I promised to put away the note block for a whole month if they let you feast with us. I told them the Great Chaos approved of all lonely people, because they could wander around and make anything happen. That it would be the most Chaotic Endermas ever if you two were there with us. And no one should be alone on Endermas. Rain could happen to anybody. It was not your fault.

Yeah, you did. Because you're a good friend. Almost as good a friend as a musician. And that was seven years ago, Kan. If you've been a human spy for seven years and no one ever even suspected, well, honestly, I think we should just make you king of the End right now, because you'd deserve it. That is a long game. We were just little babies back then. Babies can't be spies. It's ridiculous.

I guess you are right, Kan sighed.

He is, Mo agreed. *Your hubunit is just defective. That's all.*

But what about my eyes? No one else has green eyes. You have to admit, it is terribly hard to explain that away.

Neither of the twins said anything. It *was* hard to explain.

Just because we can't explain it doesn't mean it's wrong, Mo thought delicately. *It doesn't make you a monster. Some things are just different, that's all. Some fruits aren't quite the same as other fruits, some trees are a little taller or a little shorter than other trees, some cities are bigger and more beautiful, some people are . . .*

But that is just it, Mo, Kan insisted. *Some people are not. No one is different in the End. Maybe in the Overworld, what you are saying is true. But here, everyone belongs. The chorus fruits are not different colors. Some cities are not more beautiful. Everyone looks the same. Everyone is the same. Except me.*

And us, Fin added. *I guess we'll just have to be different together. Isn't that what the Great Chaos is all about? Should be all about, anyhow.*

No one thought out loud for a long while. That is to say, they were all thinking, and quite a lot, but they chose not to share it. They made their minds quiet and still as the night sky.

But you are not, Kan thought finally. *Not really. You were just like everyone else until your hubunits were caught in the rain. You are different, but your difference happened to you. And maybe when you grow up you could even fix it. You will get big and have an End of your own and you will not be different at all anymore. Everything will be fine for you. You used to be normal endermen. You will grow up into normal endermen. My eyes were never pink. And they never will be.*

I hate pink, grumped the shulker in his box. Thump-thump, thump, thump-thump.

Thanks, Grumpo, Kan thought gratefully. *Very kind of you to say.*

I hate green, too. Thump-thump, thump, thump, thump. The sound of Grumpo's box opening and shutting was uncannily like giggling. *Might bite green later.*

Kan ran his hands over a golden chestplate leaning against the side of the hold. *I just do not think we can rule it out. My being secretly human. Not yet.*

Fin threw up his hands. *Kan, just forget about it! Now, look, you can stay here as long as you want. We'll protect you. We've got plenty of weapons and some explosives so don't worry about that. But I don't want to hear any more about you being human. It's sick. Just a sick joke.*

Mo shook her head. *You can't be, you just can't be. It's not possible.*

Why not?

Because humans are terrible monsters. They're cruel and ugly and greedy. And you're . . . you're wonderful.

The twins saw the white sparkles falling slowly from end rods in their minds again. As they fell, they turned from white to red. They understood their friend was crying in frustration. He rubbed his face with his long, black fingers.

Do you not get it? I want to be human! I hope I am human! Somehow, somehow, I hope my hubunit is right. Because then everything would make sense. Suddenly, I would understand everything that has ever happened to me! My whole life would be like a story, the kind of story where in the end the person reading it thinks: Of course! It is perfect! How could I not have seen it all along? Everything would fall into place. I would know who I am. I could go somewhere and no one would look at me when I passed them on the road. No one would even care because I would be just like everyone else. I would be normal. And when I played my music, when I played . . . they would listen.

Kan kept rubbing his face, pulling hard at his cheeks. Scratching. Shoving his fingers miserably into his skin. Mo realized he wasn't rubbing at all. He was *clawing*. Clawing at the invisible pumpkin he desperately hoped was there.

Fin grabbed Kan's hands and stopped him. *Hey,* he thought gently into his friend's mind. *Don't do that. Just breathe.*

Mo jumped up. She'd remembered something. She hadn't thought of it in *ages*. Of course she hadn't, there'd never been a reason to think of it. It'd just been another bit of loot to add to the hoard. She'd found it lying next to a scorch mark that used to be a poor, dead, foolish human who must have tried to go up against ED and failed. The ender dragon had circled overhead, laughing coldly. That particular human had carried quite a lot of treasure and weapons with her into the End, which meant a good day for Mo. Where had she put it? Mo climbed over a pile of enchanted books, loose emeralds, and bows and arrows. One day they really would have to organize all this. But not today. Today, Mo remembered where she'd put things by her own mixed-up system, her own small service to the Great Chaos. Books made her think of paper, which made her think of music, emeralds made her think of Kan's eyes, and whenever she heard her friend play, she felt like an arrow had struck her in the chest. It all made sense, if you were Mo.

And there it was.

Mo pulled something hard and brown out of the mess, dislodging a lot of arrows and emeralds and several old books she fully meant to get around to reading eventually. She knelt next to Kan and put it into his hands.

Here, she thought softly. *See? Everything can be fixed. If you have your End and all its fragments. Anything can come back again.*

It was a note block.

Kan sniffled. He didn't touch it right away. He was almost afraid to. Afraid to believe it was real. Afraid to hope. His glowing spores fell around it like purple fireflies.

The young enderman let his fingers fall onto the note block. He closed his poor, tired eyes. And began to play.

CHAPTER SIX

THE FINAL BATTLE

They were all asleep when Kraj boarded their ship.

He did not come alone. Of course he didn't. Alone, who was Kraj? Nobody. Not even a cruxunit.

SOMEONE IS APPROACHING THE SHIP! Grumpo's voice exploded in Fin's, Mo's, and Kan's heads, ripping them out of a deep sleep. *A LOT OF SOMEONES ARE APPROACHING THE SHIP! WAKE UP! WAKE UP! OH, I HATE SOMEONES! WAKE UP! PROTECT ME FROM THE SOMEONES!*

The ancient cruxunit Kraj approached the stern of Fin and Mo's home surrounded by eight tall, strong endermen. Fin could see them through the portholes, drifting up over the starboard side in powerful silence. He shook his head to clear away the last of his sleep. Mo rubbed her eyes, her heart racing. Kan hung back, glaring uncertainly. None of Kraj's people opened their minds and thoughts. Their hearts were blank and dark as their long, lean bodies.

That's not Kraj's End, Fin thought, a clear, thin, laser-focused thought sent only to his friends. *I know his fragments and his sub-fragments and his sub-sub-fragments. The Great Chaos knows he has enough of them.* There was a reason Kraj was so wise, wise enough to survive so long. With an End as big as his, always around him, always underfoot, Kraj's mind was clever beyond imagining. Never unstacked. Which was why no one liked listening to him. Even endermen got annoyed with know-it-alls.

The eight endermen arranged themselves in formation around Kraj. Two stepped forward to flank the elder. The other six took up positions on the deck.

Proceed, sir, they thought in unison, a loud, hard thought very much meant to be heard over the whole of the ship. *We will protect you and prevent their escape, should they attempt to harm the one or perform the other. All hail the Great Chaos!*

May the Great Chaos smile upon you, proxy-fragments, Kraj acknowledged their obedience, utterly without emotion.

He has a new End, Mo thought, peering out at them. *They're soldiers. They're an army. A little army. Still an army.*

Fin frowned. *But we're . . . we're all on the same side. Why would Kraj bring soldiers to our ship? Why would we want to escape? Why in the world would we want to harm Kraj? If there's an army to fight the humans, we'll be in it. Won't we? Are they here to give us our orders? I don't understand what's happening.*

I do, Grumpo thought dejectedly. *You are going to hate it. I already hate it. But it is your fault because you would not let me bite even one person in the face when I told you to. Now it is going to be terrible and stupid all over you. How boring. And terrible. And stupid.*

Maybe they are here for me, Kan thought unhappily. *Maybe I am to be interrogated. Examined for evidence of pumpkin.*

Kraj and two of his bodyguards floated gracefully toward the heavy wooden door that separated the hold and the underguts of the ship from the deck.

In the name of the Great Chaos and by the command of Kraj the Ancient, open this door, fragments. Obey at once and I will treat you favorably.

If only the grown-up endermen weren't acting so strangely, the twins would have opened up without a second thought. Without a first thought. Why wouldn't they, in these terrible times? Except for Kan, they had nothing to hide.

Except for Kan.

Maybe we shouldn't, thought Mo, her hand paused above the door latch.

If we don't, they'll only break the door down. There're nine of them to three of us, Fin answered. *I don't think we've any choice.*

Well, that's just dumb, Fin. You always have a choice. Sometimes it's a garbage choice. But it's still a choice. Mo rolled her eyes at her brother. She turned to the closed door and thought as loud as she could: *If this is about Kan, you can't have him! He's not a human, we can absolutely promise you that! But if you try to take him, we really do have quite a lot of explosives on this ship. And a lot of other sharp things as well. So you might as well turn around if that's what you're up to.*

Kraj's thoughts were like hard, heavy footprints in their minds. *I am well aware of what this ship possesses. The deformed fragment is the least valuable of its contents, as I am sure you are aware. I am not his hubunit. He is irrelevant to me. As you will be if you do not open this door to your elders.*

Kan was the only thing on board that could get them in any

kind of trouble. The twins shrugged nervously and slid back the latch. They looked up into the pale old eyes of Kraj himself. But those eyes were no longer quite as faded and misty as they had been at the Endmoot. His gaze seemed quite sharp now. Sharp and fierce.

Excellent, Kraj thought as he peered into the shadows of the hold. *Just as Karshen said.* The old enderman looked keenly into Fin's eyes. *Take it all*, he ordered.

His two officers pushed into the hold with satisfaction. They immediately began going through the twins' precious, beloved loot. The soldiers lifted, examined, and commented on each item as they passed them back up out of the hold to their comrades in an orderly chain.

What are you doing? screamed Mo. *You can't! That's ours! That too! STOP! Please stop! No, that's mine, please, not my elytra, those are my oldest pair! They were on the ship when we found it! You have no right!*

One of the endersoldiers picked up a diamond axe in one hand and a crossbow in the other. She brandished both experimentally. *I think I will keep the axe for myself*, she thought approvingly. She was called Tamat. Captain Tamat. She wore her rank and name on the outside of her thoughts like a badge of pride.

Fin tried to grab it back. *No, you won't, because it's mine. I took it off a raider fair and square. I've had it all this time. You're a thief! A robber! Go get your own!* The soldier laughed and shoved him easily to the floor.

But it is my own, she sneered. *Because I took it off you fair and square. The Great Chaos works in mysterious ways!*

Kan clutched his note block to his chest and backed up slowly.

He kept backing up until his shoulders thunked against Grumpo's box, wherein Grumpo wailed pitifully.

Stealers, stealers, stealers and looters and mobs, moaned the shulker. *Go away! Go away or I will bite you. Go away AND I will bite you! EITHER WAY. BITTEN. Endermen don't use weapons! Get out!*

Kraj folded his long, shadowy fingers and turned to face them. They could feel his grin in their heads.

Our blessed Eresha, the Most High and Holy Mouth of the Great Chaos, has honored me and my long years of experience and made me commander of the armies of the End. She told me to leave no strategy unconsidered when planning our survival. Why should an enderman not use weapons? Humans use them, and we are better than they in every way. It is foolishness to leave a good sword on the ground when you could just as easily pick it up. It is my solemn duty to prepare our people for war. I was informed by— Commander Kraj glanced at Kan—*certain reliable sources that you unpleasant Endless enderfrags have been stockpiling quite the little armory out here where no one can monitor your behavioral patterns. It should never have been allowed. You are not cruxunits. You cannot just start your own group. When this is over, you will be assigned to an acceptable End and you will mature there like any other fragment. You are not special. Naturally, none of this is yours. You have lived for years on the generosity of the rest of us. Without us, without our love and compassion for your abnormal configuration, you would not have been able to collect all of this. Therefore, really, when you think about it, it was always ours. Good payment for our gentle care.*

Fin fought back tears. *You mean you left us on our own with nothing and ignored us and whispered about us and wouldn't let us stay in the city for Endermas and, and, and . . . wouldn't let us go to the Enderdome, and . . . abandoned us just because our hubunits died and . . . and never came to check on us or see if we were all right.*

I came, Kan thought quietly.

Except Kan, Fin admitted.

Commander Kraj looked puzzled. *Yes, that is just precisely what I mean. We left you alone to grow and learn and have all these riches. If anyone had asked me, I would not have permitted it. Now, I will be asked about everything, and the world will drastically improve. Endless people are dangerous. But we were kind. I do not know what you are whining about. We allowed you to exist! We could have simply exiled you to the Overworld to achieve the lofty life goal of being target practice for some human before he gets around to something more meaningful, like digging a hole in the ground. If you keep up this ungrateful complaining, perhaps I will reconsider our stance on that topic. Careful with those swords, Corporal Murrum. You are no good to the war effort if you stab yourself on the first day. Fin, Mo, your people need you. This is our darkest hour. Everyone must make sacrifices. Everyone must give something up so that the End can go on.*

Corporal Murrum finished up with the swords and bent down to pick up a large round object.

NO! Mo cried out. *Not that! Don't you dare!* She scrambled up and leapt at the other soldier like a cat. She ripped at his hands in a frenzy. *Let go of it! It's not a weapon, you don't need it! It's mine! Please, please let go!* Mo punched at Corporal Murrum's arm. He howled and almost dropped something round and greenish-blue. Mo reached for it but missed. *It's no good for anything,* she protested helplessly, furiously. *It's nothing, it's nothing except mine. Don't touch it!*

Commander Kraj jerked his head to one side sharply. He could afford to be generous. Murrum tossed the object carelessly over his shoulder. Mo leapt up frantically to catch it and held it close to her chest.

We would not leave you with nothing, he thought as the whole work of the twins' lives passed up and out of their ship, out of their home. *You can keep a few things for . . . sentimental purposes. And to defend yourselves, obviously.*

Defend ourselves? But . . . but aren't we endermen? Aren't we part of the End? We'll fight with everyone else. We'll go with you right now! Fin watched as the two soldiers turned over several books, held them upside down, smelled them, and, confused, looked to their commander for guidance.

No, I do not think we will be needing those. You cannot read a human to death. Leave them, Kraj thought. *And do not be absurd. You do not have the necessary training. There is no need for you to fight. We are not monsters! The Great Chaos does not require enderfrags as sacrifices. No, you will not fight, you will simply accompany the ender units to which I assign you in order to add your intelligence to the group and augment their abilities. You are not soldiers, my poor, innocent lambs. You are equipment. Now, what else have you got in here? Do not try to lie to me, Kraj will know. Kraj always knows.*

Mo rocked back and forth, clutching the thing she'd wrested from Corporal Murrum just as tightly as Kan clutched his note block. *If you'd only asked,* she thought through her heart breaking, *we'd have given it to you. This is our home. We want the humans defeated, too.*

Kan looked up. His green eyes went narrow and angry. *You are no better.* His thoughts were a thin, hateful hiss.

Kraj's attention cut away from the twins and refocused itself.

Only a day ago at the Endmoot he'd seemed like such a kind old enderman. Now all that was gone. *Pardon me, fragment? No better than whom?*

Humans! Kan snapped. *You come here and take what you want without asking, without caring, only thinking of yourself and what you can use. You are invading this ship just like they are invading the End. Looting my friends. Ruining their home. Taking, taking, taking. Humans take and take until they cannot even carry everything they stole. They are like big angry horses. They eat and eat because they are too stupid to know their stomachs are about to explode. And that is what you are like too. So I do not see why we should be equipment for anyone if we are going to be eaten no matter which dumb horse is doing the chewing.*

Kraj narrowed his glowing eyes. *How fascinating. You have so much empathy and insight into human beings, young Kan. I wonder where you found all this intimate knowledge of the species? Where this wonderful clarity could possibly have come from? Perhaps I was too hasty in calming your hubunit's fears.*

No, Fin thought quickly. *It's fine. It's just stuff.* He felt sick. He felt like he was going to throw up. *Just junk.* He watched Captain Tamat gather up a dozen different kinds of arrows—Arrows of Regeneration, of Fire Resistance, of Poison, Spectral Arrows, Arrows of Water Breathing, even his precious Arrows of the Turtle Master. She grabbed them like they were all the same, just a bunch of identical sticks, and shoved them out of the hold like firewood, toward the rest of the ender squad.

Take it, Mo joined her twin. *We want to help. We were only saying you could have asked. That's all.*

That is what I suspected. Poor Endless trashfrags. You will find that in periods of war, niceties are a waste of time as you are a waste of ender flesh. *And almost everything is niceties, in the end. In the End as well! Ah, how marvelous it feels to be in the company of my squad. I feel my brain practically sizzle with intellect. Wordplay! Can you imagine? If only the war had come years ago!*

Thump-thump, thump. Grumpo's box thudded meekly.

Commander Kraj waved his hand dismissively toward the stern of the ship. *Do not bother, shulker. You hate me. I am aware.*

I hope a human eats your eyes, Grumpo whispered. *I really mean that.*

The hold was almost empty. The books remained in a tottering tower in the corner, and a few torches. Two or three swords and a few scattered pieces of armor lay on the floor. Fin watched them congratulate one another on a job well done. *But why do you need our chorus fruits and carrots and cooked mutton? What can you do against a human with that?*

We are hungry, thought the corporal and the captain.

So are we, thought the three enderfrags together.

Why should I care? Captain Tamat thought as she climbed the stairs into the open air. *What are you the captain of?*

You had better find some food then, had you not? Corporal Murrum added, somewhat more kindly. But not much more.

Our business is concluded, little fragments, Commander Kraj announced.

Not really that little, Mo sniffed.

Compared to me, you are infinitesimally tiny. Mind your manners or I will cut them out of you. Report to the central island at midnight for your assignments. We have left plenty for you to outfit yourselves, so I expect you to present yourselves in tip-top shape, understood?

They glanced around at the barren hold. Suddenly Grumpo's

box had an echo when it thumped. Kraj stared mercilessly into their unhappy faces.

Enough. You did not deserve such luxuries and you would have no idea what to do with golden swords, which is handily proven by the fact that all you did with them while you had them was serve each other lunch. We have left you items befitting your station in life. Be grateful.

Mo, Fin, and Kan glowered silently.

I said be grateful, soldiers! Or by the Great Chaos, I will make you grateful!

Thank you, Commander Kraj, they thought in a shaky, resentful unison.

That is better. Midnight. If you shirk your duty, I shall personally tell the first human I meet where you are and how good you taste. And if I hear one more word of empathy out of you, young man, I shall happily let the medics dissect you to see if you really are an enderman all the way through to your bones.

And then they were gone. All nine of them, as though a storm had hit the ship and passed on, leaving only wreckage.

Kan stared after the commander. *I remember when Kraj gave me a roasted endermite all to myself to eat at Endermas. He told me I was a handsome lad. He told me a funny story about something from the Overworld called a pig.*

I don't think he means to bounce anyone on his knee anymore, Mo shuddered.

Funny what the word "commander" can do to a person, Fin grumbled.

I hate him, Grumpo huffed without so much as lifting the lid of his box.

For once, I think we all agree with you, Grumps, Mo thought. Kan patted the shulker's box.

Pigs are pink, the green-eyed enderman thought. *Pigs are pink and they eat mud. That is what Kraj said.*

Fin and Mo frowned. That didn't sound right, but they didn't much feel like correcting their friend. It wasn't the time for that.

Well, what have we got left? Kan thought after a long, unhappy session of staring into the nothingness of their future.

Fin sighed. *A damaged wooden sword, a Loyalty trident— I think Tamat stepped on it. A crossbow, a leather tunic for each of us, and it looks like we'll have to fight over who gets the enchanted one. Ooh, a damaged stone sword, how posh! A lot of books, your note block, some crappy potions that didn't get completely dumped out, exactly one bowl of chorus fruit, and whatever Mo decided to make such a fuss about.*

The boys kept a respectful distance, but they were dying to see what she'd hit an enderman, a full-grown endersoldier to save.

Mo sat on the floor of the hold. She hadn't moved a muscle the whole time. Just sat there, immobile with rage, holding on to . . . that thing. The thing Corporal Murrum had tried to take. That round, greenish-blue thing that had been so important to her.

It's nothing, she thought, the white lights of her tears glittering in her friends' minds like snow. *It's stupid. I don't know why, I just lost my mind when I saw him tossing it around. He could have broken it.*

Fin leaned in. *What is it, Mo?*

Mo stroked the thing in her arms fondly. *It's mine. It's so mine I didn't even tell you about it. I found it last summer. ED showed me.*

The ender dragon gave you something? Kan couldn't believe it. That great huge beast never did anything for anyone.

Not exactly. Not gave. It showed me. Under the island. Someone must have dropped it. Or maybe it just spawned there. Like magic. Like fate. She shook her head. *But I told you. It's stupid. I always thought it would . . . do something. But it never did.* Mo pulled her long black arms away to reveal a large, slightly moldy, greenish-bluish-purplish-yellowish egg lying in her lap. *I thought, you know, if I kept it warm in the hold with all the torches and everything, it might hatch.*

Fin sat back on his heels. *What in the name of the Great Chaos is* that?

It's a zombie horse egg, Mo confessed. *And now it's cracked.*

CHAPTER SEVEN

HUMANS

Midnight came.

And went.

The endermen gathered as one nation on the ender dragon's gorgeous barren island. They stood in formation beneath the obsidian pillars topped with crystal flames in silver cages. They stood wearing Fin's and Mo's life's work. All their belongings, stuck awkwardly onto everybody else whether any of it fit or not. The younger endermen ran between units, carrying supplies and orders, lending their intellects to the group, trying to find the right balance of minds for war. Mo was assigned to a flank of archers. Commander Kraj attached Fin far away, to a healing unit. But no matter what they said to his face, no one trusted Kan enough to take him, so he hung back, on the outside looking in, as he'd always been. Only this time, he was clutching a damaged stone sword like it could save his life.

The Great Ender Army turned their violet eyes to the night, ready to lay down their lives for the End. The ender dragon circled above them, roaring fire and hate and vengeance and death to all humans.

They were ready.

It was so quiet they could hear one another breathing in the dark. So quiet they could feel the steady song of the ender pearls inside each and every one of them. Never had so many endermen come together like this. Their intelligence crackled between them like electricity. In that moment, if not for the terrible purpose that had gathered them, the unified nation of endermen could have solved any problem put to them. They could have invented any fantastical machine. If the wisest creature alive in the universe had asked them the most difficult, mystical philosophical riddle, the endermen could have answered it in three or four seconds. That was how clever they were when they were one vast End, which they never had been before, nor would be again.

The air thrummed with anticipation. It was the kind of quiet that happens only before an incredible storm, before an unimaginable catastrophe. Before war.

And nothing happened.

Eventually, everyone went home. People were hungry. They were tired. They were even a little bored. They just didn't know what else they were supposed to do. They had scheduled a war. If the humans had decided not to show up, the endermen supposed that they'd won by default. But had they won? They couldn't be quite sure.

———

The ship was deathly quiet when Mo and Fin and Kan returned to it. They stood on the deck for a while. A little confused. A little upset. And a little, even though none of the three of them wanted to admit it, *disappointed*. It wasn't that they *wanted* to go to war. Wars were dangerous. You could die in wars. Bits of you could become separated from the rest. Not just arms and legs, either. Souls. Hearts. Memories. But when you've gotten yourself hot and brave enough to do something, and don't get to actually *do* it, there is a very strange hole leftover where you so nicely stacked up all that bravery to begin with.

Unfortunately, constant telepathy means never getting to completely hide how you feel. They knew they were all feeling the same odd disappointment. They knew they all felt they shouldn't be disappointed that they weren't going to get to kill all humans today. And yet the ship never stopped being as quiet as guilt.

The twins faced the prospect of their empty home. They stared down into the shadowy hold. Torches flickered on the walls. At least they hadn't taken those. Grumpo's box sat resentfully silent against the far back wall. Mo had somehow hoped that it would be magically full again. But of course it wasn't. The purple and yellow wood of the ship, wood they hadn't seen in years, practically shone in all the places where blocks and chests and boxes had protected it from dirt and footprints. Except for the mountain of books the army hadn't wanted, it was unsettlingly clean.

Like Grumpo, they hated it.

Fin, Mo thought with a panic. *We're poor. We don't have anything to eat. We don't have gold. We don't have anything. How are we going to live?*

Fin frowned. *Maybe they'll bring it all back in a day or two. Apologize. Maybe Kraj will tell us some more stories about pigs.*

Pigs are pink, Kan thought distractedly.

Fin nodded. *So they say.*

No, but I'm serious. What are we going to eat? What I mean is, what are we going to eat tonight? Right now? I'm starving.

Can you eat books? Mo rubbed her dark belly. *I suppose we can, but would it help? Are books nutritious? Maybe they have . . . good fats. Or something.*

Don't you dare. Fin was shocked. Books were the closest thing he had to training in the Enderdome like the others. Learning. Studying the enemy. *They're all we've got left. Why don't we eat your egg then? At least eggs are food! Zombie horses are way more likely to have good fats! Yum, yum, yum!*

Mo raced to the corner where she'd hidden her egg. She cradled it tenderly in her arms. She examined the crack. It didn't seem to have grown any wider while she'd been gone. *That's so mean. Why are you being mean? If you touch my egg, I'll touch you.*

Fin felt bad immediately. He hadn't meant it. Well, he mostly hadn't meant it. He was *very* hungry and it was a *rather* big egg even if it was also a zombie. It was only that she'd said she was going to eat the books! *Sorry, Mo. I'm sorry. I guess I've got some mean stored up that was supposed to get used on the war and now it just . . . wants to get used any old way it can.*

Mo glared at him and held her egg tighter.

Suddenly, Grumpo's box clapped open and shut. Three times, very quick. They all jumped nearly out of their skins. Three apples flew out of the shulker's lair and thudded onto the floor.

GRUMPO! Fin's and Mo's minds sang out joyfully. They dashed down to snatch up the food.

WHO'S A GOOD BOY? Mo kissed the front of his box all over. The shulker snarled inside.

Not me. I'm not. They're poison. Get away from me.

No, they're not, Fin laughed. *They're good apples and you're a good boy, YES, YOU ARE.*

Very brave of you, to hide something from Commander Kraj, Kan marveled.

I didn't. You can't prove it. I hope you choke, spluttered Grumpo, and then he refused to think anything more at all while the twins called him so many sweet names and said so many nice things about him that the shulker vomited twice in his box. And shulker vomit is not very nice at all.

The three of them stuck the apples onto the ends of their swords and roasted their little feast in the torchlight. Maybe their last feast for a good while. They'd have to start all over again. Start collecting fruits and flowers from the chorus trees like they had when they were little. Like Endless beggars.

They didn't feel very full when they'd finished their apples. In fact, they felt somewhat ill and very sleepy. A shulker is a shulker in the end, and the apples actually were a *little* poisoned. But it was only one apple apiece, for better (still hungry) and worse (slightly poisoned). Mo, Fin, and Kan finally fell asleep sitting up on the hard floor of the ship's hold, back to back to back. Mo curled around her egg, Kan curled around his note block, Fin curled up beside his books. They were exhausted. For the first time any of them could remember, they had no idea what was going to happen next. They dreamed of apples, and pigs, and music, and hubunits, and a rain that could come anytime, even when the sky was clear.

The whispers came hours later. In the absolute dead of night. All hours in the End can be called "the absolute dead of night" but this really was. The end rods were at their dimmest. Total quiet and darkness everywhere you could look or listen—and then.

Whispers.

Outside the door. On the ship's deck. Soft, secret, urgent.

Mo woke up first. Her heart thundered in her head. They'd already taken everything! Why would they come back! She moved protectively in front of her brother and her friend. She hid her egg behind her back. Maybe Kraj had decided she couldn't keep that either.

More whispers. Louder now.

Now Fin woke up. His magenta eyes slitted open in the half-dark.

Someone's out there, Mo told him.

Kan sat up. *Is it my hubunits? Karshen? Teg?*

I don't think so. Mo glanced toward the stern and the shulker's ledge. *I wonder why Grumpo isn't yelling his head off.*

The whispers were right outside the door now. Something knocked hard against the wood. They could almost make out words.

Fin and Mo realized it at the same time. Their eyes got big and wide.

What? Kan looked back and forth between them, not under-standing.

Whispers, Mo thought.

Yes, I hear them, too. Is it Kraj? Corporal Murrum? Captain Tamat?

Mo grabbed his hand and squeezed hard. Then she pressed his hand to the side of his head. *Yeah, Kan, you do. You* hear *them. With* your *ears.*

Someone outside the ship was talking. Not with telepathy. No beautiful thoughts appearing gracefully and instantly in another person's mind. Talking. With their *faces*. A lot of faces. Grumpo wasn't alerting them because Grumpo didn't *know*. The shulker couldn't sense other minds approaching the ship because the people approaching the ship weren't telepathic. Their minds were shut. Their mouths were open.

"Shhhhhh! You klutz."

"Why? Afraid I'll startle the loot?"

"It's another big dumb ship like all the other big dumb ships. Get in there, kill the shulker, open the chests, grab the elytra, get out. Lather, rinse, repeat."

"I don't know. It's creepy here. It's so *quiet*. Just be careful."

"We can go back to the dragon if you want. He wasn't quiet."

"You don't know it's a he."

"Oh my god, are we gonna raid this place or not?"

"Fine."

"Fine."

"You first."

"Whatever. God, you're such a *baby*, Roary."

The endermen stared at the closed door in horror.

Humans.

Here.

Now.

And they had no escape.

The door slammed open. Four *things* poured into the ship. Blocky, hulking, squat, splotchy creatures. Their skin was all different colors when it should have been nice and slick and black. Their clothes were different colors, too—one wore red, one wore turquoise, one wore green, and one wore yellow. *And they were wearing clothes!* Any kind of clothes! An enderman's skin was skin and shirt and coat and trousers and armor all in one. They'd never seen clothes. Ever. Chestplates, sure. But jeans and T-shirts? Fin and Mo didn't even know the words for those things. They didn't seem like they'd be much good as armor. What was the point of them?

The human mob yelled and brandished their weapons. They hurtled into Fin and Mo's private space, their home, laughing and swinging their swords crazily, barely even looking at what they might hit. The one in the turquoise shirt threw herself at Kan. She held a diamond sword high above her head and slashed it down toward him with a yodeling war cry. Sobbing, Mo hit the human hard in the stomach, knocking her back before she could cut off Kan's head.

"Ugh," the human grunted. "I hate these guys. So annoying."

"Ooh!" said the human girl in red. "That one's got green eyes! *Coooool.*"

Stay away from him! Mo lashed back. But the girl couldn't hear a thought any more than she could hear a memory.

I'm fine, Kan thought shakily. *She didn't get me. I've got my sword still.* He groped behind himself for it and found the handle.

Mo fixed the wicked human girls with the terrible gaze of the endermen. Once an enderman has her prey in her line of sight, nothing can stop her. An all-consuming berserker fury takes over and it does not fade until the target is torn to pieces.

But the girls didn't seem to notice that they'd been fixed with the terrible gaze of the endermen. They whispered something to each other and ignored Mo completely.

The boy in the yellow shirt ran up to Grumpo and started whacking his box all over with a trident. A trident! Fin couldn't help admiring it, he'd only ever found one and Kraj had almost made off with it. Tridents were his favorite. He'd always hoped he'd find another one, but he never did. He charged the human in yellow, throwing himself between him and Grumpo. The trident hit him in the shoulder, in the knee, and glanced off his elbow, which somehow hurt worse than the others.

"Get out of the way!" the yellow human snarled at Fin. "I don't have time for you!"

Please leave us alone, wailed Fin. His arm hurt so bad. He kept trying to look the boy in the eye, to fill himself up with that all-powerful, undeniable frenzy that was the legacy of his people. His birthright. But the human didn't seem to care about legacies and he couldn't hear Fin's thoughts. All the human could see was an enderman flashing red with pain and rage, who didn't immediately charge him or bludgeon him to death.

Grumpo was most certainly awake now. He was so angry, his thoughts couldn't even form themselves into words, just one long scream of hate like a knife dragging through their heads.

KIIIIIIIIIILLLLLLLLLL IIIIIIIIT! shrieked the shulker.

"What the actual crap," said the human boy in green. "There's frick-all in here. Not even one chest? Worst. Boat. Ever. Koal, dude, are you really having trouble taking out a *shulker*? That's like baby's-first-kill territory. *Weak*. Leave it alone, I think you're just *bothering* it now."

"Let's go, Jax," the girl in red sighed. "This is stupid. And pointless. Somebody else obviously got here first."

"Yeah, sorry, guys," the girl in the blue shirt who'd tried to decapitate Kan apologized. "We didn't know anyone else was raiding this far out. Our bad. I'm Roary, this is Jesster"—she jabbed her thumb back at her red friend—"the big guy is Jax and the skinny one's Koal."

Who are they talking to? Mo thought wildly. She squeezed her egg to her chest. Somehow that made her feel better. *Is this the invasion?*

I don't know! Fin panted heavily, his arm still burning in agony. He turned from one human to the other, his hands curled into claws, ready to fight again.

Jax made a face. "Kind of weird to just be *hanging out* in here with an enderman, but you do you, I guess," he said. "Did you kill the dragon yet? If not, you're welcome to come with us. Once I'm looted up, I'm gonna stab that bad boy in the heart."

"Hey," said Jesster, snapping her fingers. "Helllloooo? Rude! Aren't you gonna say something? You can still talk with a pumpkin on, you know."

Kan's bright, beautiful green eyes widened. *They are talking to me,* he thought. *I am human. I was human all along. They think I raided this boat. Like them. Like a normal human boy. They think I raided this boat and tricked you into thinking I was a harmless enderman. And I guess . . . I guess they are right.*

Kan took a step toward the humans. The look on his face was so horribly happy and sad all at once. He opened his mouth to talk, really talk, no silky, silent thoughts. Not anymore. Real words. Human words. At last.

"Whoa, Jess!" Koal called out. "Look out! It's coming right for you!"

Koal lunged forward and swung his trident. It caught Kan on the cheek. The wound flared red, but it wasn't deep. The green-eyed enderman stared at the humans, full of hurt and confusion.

"You guys should probably just kill him," the one called Jax said. "Sneaking around is pretty fun, not gonna lie, but it's easier just to clear the zone first thing. Don't worry, they won't even see you coming. They're too stupid to breathe. As long as you've got your pumpkin, you can kill 'em left and right and they still won't figure out what's up."

Fin and Mo just stood there, gawping. Grumpo was still screaming in their heads, like he was trying to drown out the intolerable sound of the humans talking. The place where they'd stacked up their bravery was clean cleared out. They didn't understand. Maybe they didn't want to understand. The twins grabbed each other's hands.

Please just go away and let this not be happening, Fin thought.

Maybe we're still asleep. Maybe the apples really were poisoned. Maybe Grumpo IS a bad boy. Always knew he might be, Mo thought, her mind starting to break under the pressure. She held on to her egg. Her egg was solid. Her egg was real. The egg was love. The egg was life.

Roary cleared her throat. "Awkward."

"Anyway . . ." Jax coughed. "You two want to come kill a dragon? Us humans gotta stick together, you know."

Us humans? the twins thought. *Two?*

Kan crumpled to the floor.

Grumpo's telepathic scream cut off sharply.

Fin clung to his sister.

Mo squeezed her egg as tight as she could, tight enough to make it all go away.

The egg cracked.

CHAPTER EIGHT

THE SIX OF US

You're mistaken, thought Fin angrily. *We're not human.*

Something long and thin and greyish-violet broke the shell of the egg. It had a hard, yellow hoof on one end, like a fist made all out of old thumbnail.

You have got it wrong, thought Kan desperately. *It is me. I am the one. I am human.*

A second spindly skinny thing emerged from Mo's egg. Bloodshot veins snaked all over it in a complicated pattern that looked almost like the design on a pretty vase, only much, much gorier and . . . wetter.

What in the name of the Great Chaos do you mean "kill a dragon with you"? Mo thought accusingly. *I hope you don't mean ED because it will burn you standing.*

Something very big was trying very hard to be born out of her egg. The spindly legs wiggled in the air with effort. The head pushed at the bluish-green shell. A sickly looking head with bits of bright bone showing through the bruised-looking skin. A head with sharp yellow teeth. A head with mold on it before it even took its first breath.

The thing neighed.

The neigh sounded like a coffin opening.

It looked up into Mo's dark, loving face with enormous dark eyes fringed with funguslike eyelashes.

Mumma? the zombie horse croaked in the space between their minds.

"Wow! I heard about those!" Jesster exclaimed. "The eggs are super tough to find! I'll trade you a nether star for it."

Mo wrapped her arms protectively around the undead horse's neck. It was a girl. A mare. Her hair was stringy and moist and smelled like raw beef.

Mumma, the ghoul burped happily. Her breath put out a torch. *Brains. Braaaains?* the zombie foal sniffed around for that special food all zombies love. She fixed her bloodshot eyes meaningfully on Fin's head.

Your baby is disgusting, Grumpo observed from his box. *I hate it. You should put it in the garbage. I can smother it for you if you want.*

Put yourself in the garbage! Mo snapped back. *She's beautiful! Aren't you, baby?*

Mo, don't you think there're more important things going on right now?

Mo glared at her brother stubbornly. *No.* Very gently, she kissed the horse's forehead. *You're all I have left,* she thought softly. *You're my whole old life if my old life was a stinky horse. I don't want whatever is about to happen to us to happen and I don't want to know whatever we're about to know, but you can't stop things happening and you can't unknow something once you know it, so I'm just going to focus on this until it stops happening. I'm never gonna let you go. You have the prettiest sores.*

Mo had no idea what the mind of a zombie horse was like. She'd heard her thoughts, so telepathy was on the table. But could a dead mind even open up enough to fully let someone else's thoughts in? Mo considered it silently. There was no way to know except to try. She smiled at the creature and tried to see inside her brain, her mind, her soul. Mo pushed her mind toward the pony's mind.

She saw a graveyard. It went on forever, over a hundred hills and more. All the dirt was freshly turned. Wiry, crooked trees bent over the tombs. A sickly white moon shone on all of it. Nothing seemed to respond to her thoughts. The gravestones said various things: HELLO. HI. BEAUTIFUL. DISGUSTING. BABY. PUT IT IN THE GARBAGE. WOW. BRAINS. MUMMA. HUNGRY. HUNGRY. HUNGRY. MUMMA. BRAINS. Most of them were blank, though. Not that much had happened to her yet, after all.

A bloated, rotting hand slowly wiggled its way out of one of the graves. The fingernails were fuzzy with purple-black mold. Worms squirmed out of a hole in the palm.

The gravestone above it read: HELLO.

It waved shyly at Mo.

Hi, baby, Mo thought.

"HEY!" yelled Koal. "It's. Very. Rude. To. Give. Nice. People. The. Silent. Treatment." He clapped his hands between each word.

"Mouth go like this," Jax said in an exaggerated slow voice.

He reached out and wiggled Fin's jaw mockingly.

Fin's jaw came off in his hand.

Mo screamed. Not in her head. Not in Fin's head. Not in Kan's head.

She *screamed*. The sound echoed around the ship's hold. The zombie horse screamed, too, in exactly the same pitch, but with a lot more volume. Learning was fun, even for demon ponies.

But it wasn't Fin's jaw.

It was a piece of pumpkin.

In the beautiful black shell of the enderman's face, a shard of warm brown skin showed through.

Jax held it casually in his hand like nothing unusual had happened. "Ew," he said. "Your pumpkin is nasty. It's all old and rotty. I don't know how much longer it's gonna last, buddy."

No, Fin thought, staring at Mo. *It's impossible*.

"What's that, friend?" said Roary encouragingly. "Once more with volume?"

"Impossible," Fin wheezed. His voice was creaky and raw and harsh and husky. Like it hadn't been used in years. Because it hadn't.

Mo raised her hand to her own face. She felt like she was in a trance. The enderman wedged her fingers under her jaw, exactly where Jax had grabbed Fin. She tried to lift up.

A slice of pumpkin shell came away like rotted wood.

Mo dropped it like it was on fire. It fell to the ground. One side still looked black and shiny. The other oozed soft, gooshy, spoiled pumpkin. It even had a couple of seeds sticking out of it. After a moment, the piece of pumpkin shriveled up into dust and disappeared.

Kan raised his hand to his cheek. He slid his fingers under his jaw. He lifted it upward.

Nothing happened.

No, he moaned in his mind. *No, no, no. It's impossible.*

He kept pulling at his face. Kept lifting, kept scrabbling along the line of his jaw to find the edge of the pumpkin mask. The mask that wasn't there. Tears filled his mind. *It does not make any sense. I am the one. It is me. It is not them. Please, please be me.*

"I don't . . . I don't understand what's happening here," Fin said. It was so *hard* to talk! So many muscles! So many different movements! "Can you talk, Mo?"

Mo tried to open her mouth. Her *other* mouth. The mouth underneath the face she'd thought was her real face for all these years. "I . . . I think so," she whispered hoarsely. "It hurts."

Mumma. Paaaain, moaned the undead horse in her arms. Her mouth didn't move, but Fin and Kan heard it, too. Mo stroked the baby's forehead.

See, Grumpo? she thought. *She's not disgusting. She knows when I hurt and she cares, which is more than you've ever done.* The horse began to *gurgle* happily, almost like a purr, if the purr came from hell itself.

Kan lay down on the floor of the ship. He couldn't move. He couldn't think. His brain just wouldn't *brain.*

"Um . . . you're people. Who found a couple of pumpkins and used them to raid the End without getting attacked every five seconds by an enderman with an anger-management problem," Jesster told them impatiently. "Duh."

"But that's not true," insisted Mo. Her throat ached with the effort of talking. And the more she *talked* instead of *thought,* the more she knew that they were right. "We've always lived here. I can't even remember any other place. We grew up here. It's our home. It was our hubunits' home. We're endermen." She said it again, trying to hold on to everything she'd ever known about herself. "We're endermen."

We're endermen.

"I mean . . . except for the part where you're not," Koal said, almost laughing at them.

"What's a hubunit?" Jess asked, confused.

"We *are* endermen! We are so!" Fin tried to shout, but his voice wasn't up to it yet.

"Okay, crazy," Jax rolled his eyes. "Have it your way. We're out."

"Wait," Roary said, holding up her hands. "Wait a minute. This is so interesting. Do you really not know? Do you not remember how you got here?"

"We were born here!" sobbed Mo.

Koal stuck his hands into his yellow pockets. "Fine. Where're your parents?"

"What's a *parent*?" Mo blurted in frustration.

Jess blinked. Roary blinked. Koal opened his mouth to say something, then shut it again and furrowed his brow. Jax laughed—a short, sharp, harsh sound more like a cough than a laugh. "You know, your parents. Like . . . a mom and a dad."

"What's a mom?" Fin asked.

"What's a dad?" asked Mo.

"How can you not know what a mom and dad are?" Jess said incredulously. "The people who look like you only bigger and talk like you only louder, who make the rules and bad jokes and say things like 'Not under my roof,' and 'What time do you call this?' and 'We love you very much but you can't have cake for breakfast.' The people who made you!"

"Hubunits," said Mo.

"Mom and dad," insisted Koal.

"Primary and secondary hubunits," Mo allowed.

Mumma! the zombie horse thought triumphantly.

Roary rolled her eyes. "Okay, okay, what happened to your primary and secondary hubunits?"

"They died," Fin mumbled. "A long time ago."

Kan's green eyes slid open. His brain perked up a little. It might, just maybe, have been willing to brain again. Temporarily.

Did they? He sent the thought toward his friends. *Did they, though?*

Of course they did! Fin snarled, whipping his head around in bitterness.

How dare you? Mo thought. The baby monster in her lap glared at Kan.

All right. Kan's thought was very small and simple. *What is your primary hubunit's name?*

Mo blinked.

How about your secondary hubunit?

Fin opened his mouth to say, but he . . . couldn't. He reached back to all his memories of their End, of their childhood. But . . . it just wasn't there.

"Hey!" Jax snapped his fingers in their faces to get their attention. "What's going on here? Are you having an episode? You guys just keep stopping and staring off into the distance. Do you have a glitch? Do you need help? You need a healing potion or something?"

"Sorry," Fin croaked. "We're talking."

"No, you're not," countered Jesster.

"Yes, we are. We're endermen. Or *whatever* we are. Endermen communicate telepathically. That's what all the little purple sparkles are about." Roary reached out to touch one. It danced out of range. "They let us send our thoughts directly into other endermen's minds. Shulkers, too, if they're willing, which they almost never are. We're talking to our friend there. His name is Kan. I'm Mo. This is my twin, Fin."

"You're *friends* with an *enderman?*" Roary said in total disbelief. "You can't be friends with an enderman."

"We're friends with *lots* of endermen," Mo said defensively. All the more defensively because they absolutely were *not* friends with lots of endermen. But the humans didn't need to know they were the village losers. "Anyway, I think maybe he's . . . like us? Whatever we are?" All right, they were *something*. Something different. But not *humans*. That was too horrible to entertain. Mo took her hand off the purring colt and stroked poor Kan's miserable head. Her fingers left wet, dark marks on his temples. Her new horse was a messy horse. Kan didn't mind. He didn't mind much of anything anymore. What was the point of minding?

"Nope," Koal shook his head. "That's an enderman. A real one. They're *pretty* easy to pick out of a lineup."

"Maybe," Mo said doubtfully. "But he's different, too."

"The eyes," Roary mused. "I've never seen eyes like that on an enderman. Anywhere. Ever."

"I bet you want to rip them out for your next portal, huh?" Mo said.

Jax thought about it, then shrugged. "Nah, we're already here. We're good. You only need eyes for the . . . er . . . outgoing call. And I don't think you need actual—"

"Okay, but back to the actually interesting thing," Roary interrupted. She seemed terribly fascinated by them. Almost like a doctor. You could tell she was just dying to examine them, figure them out, maybe even dissect them. "How can you be human and not remember being human? How long have you been down here? What happened to you? Jax, do we know any Fins or Mos that have gone missing? What if we take the pumpkins all the way off? Maybe their memories will come back."

No, Kan's thought flashed. *No, do not do it. If you take them off, everyone will know. They will attack you.*

You're not attacking us now.

And he wasn't. Kan didn't know why he wasn't. But he wasn't attacking anyone in a room jam-packed full of humans. He didn't even want to. What was wrong with him? Just how much of a freak *was* he?

"This sucks," announced Jax. "Can he talk?"

"I told you, endermen communicate telepathically," Fin began again.

"Yeah, yeah, yeah, psychic monster people. Got it. But *can* he talk? I can talk, but I can *also* think. Ipso . . . you know."

"Facto," Roary finished for him. "You dolt."

Mo put her head to one side. "I guess I don't know." She turned to her friend.

Kan, can you try to talk?

I am talking.

Talk like the humans talk. Can you just try? It's pretty easy. Once you get used to it. You move the bottom of your face up and down and kind of . . . breathe out loud.

"Come on, buddy," Jax said, like he was talking to a big, mean dog who would bite if he didn't get a treat. "Give us a nice talky-talk."

Kan glowered. "No," he rumbled.

But it was so hard for him. His mouth was so little compared to the humans' mouths. You couldn't even see it unless he opened it as far as it could go. His tongue didn't know how to do much of anything besides eat. Words *hurt* coming out of him. Hurt like knives.

"I bet you're fun at parties." Jax sighed. "Look, you can't chatty-chat-chat with us and then be all woo-woo-spooky-mind-meld with him. Manners, people."

Mo wrinkled her nose. Now that she knew it was there, the pumpkin made her face itch. How had she never noticed?

"You're kind of awful," she said to the big boy in the green shirt. He grinned. It didn't bother him.

"Yeah, but he's our awful." Koal sighed.

"I might be awful but I'm not wrong! It's rude. And it puts us at a disadvantage."

"Again, I would like to stress that this situation is possibly unique in the *history of the world*," Roary said. "They've been lost in Monster Central for maybe years. We've got to figure this out. At the very least, you guys, we can take you out of here. We can take you *home*."

"Once we kill the dragon," Koal reminded her.

"Yes, obviously we can't go anywhere until Jax has his little dragon party, but after that, we can take you all back up with us."

Jess crossed her arms and didn't say anything. Fin realized he was staring at her. He hadn't meant to. He was so used to living in a telepathic world that he hadn't even noticed he was concentrating hard on Jess, waiting for her thoughts to appear in his mind. They didn't. She was a closed book. Whatever was making her frown and stare off into the distance, Fin couldn't just *know* it. It was frustrating and horrible and he realized he must look really odd glaring at her like that and yanked his gaze away. How did humans live like that? Anyone could just keep secrets from you and you'd never know!

Mumma remaaaaaain, howled the undead pony in the grave-yard of her mind, and snuggled into Mo's chest defensively. To the animal, this was home. She had been alive for only half an hour. She wasn't ready to move to a new neighborhood yet.

"Are you gonna keep that thing?" Koal said, wrinkling his nose. The smell was overpowering. "Like, as a pet?"

MUMMA, barked the horse silently. Red spittle flew from her teeth.

"She's my baby," Mo said lovingly.

"Gross," Jax said. He covered his mouth and dry heaved. A long, empty, gutteral burp came out.

"She's not *gross.* She's *mine.* I'm going to call her Loathsome. Isn't that a nice name for a nice horse who definitely will not eat my brains the minute I'm not looking? Definitely not, right?"

Naaaaame, Loathsome thought lovingly. In that endless cemetery in her head, one of the gravestones suddenly read: LOATH-SOME. She snatched up Mo's hand in her rotting yellow fangs. Mo gasped. Her heart stopped. But Loathsome just held her fingers very gently, as if to say: *I could, but I won't. But I* could. The zombie horse made a churning, crunching, bubbling sound in her decomposing throat. A giggle.

"Wow," said Koal, shaking his head. He raised his hands as if to say: It's your funeral. "Just *wow.*"

"Shut up!" Mo snarled. "And you better not still be thinking about fighting the ender dragon, because if you have to kill it to get home you might as well start building a nice house here in the End. I won't let you hurt my dragon."

"Your dragon?" said Jax softly.

"Well . . . not mine exactly. Not anyone's exactly. But I love it, and that makes it mine."

"That's not how love works," Jess broke her silence.

"Fine! But I'm not going to let you kill it, because it's beautiful and unique and it breathes fire and knows my name. I'll fight you to the end of the End to keep it safe and I'm pretty sure that *is* how love works."

"We are not going to the Overworld." Fin snapped them all back to attention. "And neither are you. I don't think you're to-tally aware of everything that's going on here. We knew you were coming. Everyone knew. We were ready for you. We just . . . thought you were coming earlier. And that there would be more of you."

"When they find out you're already here, Commander Kraj will bring the greatest army the End has ever known down on your heads. There're only four of you. You won't survive."

"Six of us," said Jesster gently. "Six humans here, kittens."

"What are you talking about?" Roary said. "Endermen don't have armies. They don't have commanders. What is going *on* down here?"

"We do now." Mo shrugged.

"Ooh, I'm shaking in my enchanted boots," said Jax, waggling his fingers. "I came here to kill a dragon and I don't care how many of your weird freakshow countrymen I have to go through to do it. We're better than them. Endermen are annoyingly strong, but it's not like they're particularly smart. I've always done just fine against them."

Kan strained, moving his jaw unnaturally, trying to speak. Fi-nally, he spat out his words. "Not a freak," he coughed up like sickness. "Not a freak."

"Okay, greenboy, you're not a freak. Happy?"

Kan screamed. His skin flushed red. He bolted at Jax and threw him against the port-side wall. The ship groaned in the sky.

"Get off me! Get off me!"

Koal grabbed Fin by the shoulder. "Call off your friend or I'll stab him in the back," the human boy warned. "I mean it. You care about him, but I don't. I care about Jax."

"Kan, stop!" Fin shouted. "Stop it!"

The enderman stopped. It was so hard to stop. But he did it. He did it because Fin said to. Fin knew the right thing to do almost all of the time. He always had. Since they were small. But had they grown up together? Was it all a lie? What was *happening*?

Roary put her hands on her hips. "I think the first thing to do is get the pumpkins off. It might help. You might remember everything. I don't really know how those things work. We found them growing in patches and started screwing around because it was a boring day and it turned out they were just . . . *massively* useful. Maybe if you wear them too long they mess with your head. It could make sense."

"But the others . . ."

"Don't worry, you can put them back on if anyone turns up," the girl reassured them.

"Grumpo would tell us if anyone was approaching. Any enderman, anyway," Mo said uncertainly. *Would* Grumpo warn them? He was suspiciously silent. Maybe he wouldn't talk to them anymore, now that he knew they were outsiders. She picked a few stray pieces of eggshell off her pony. The pony was already much bigger. She had been the size of a chicken when she hatched. Now she was about the size of a dog.

"I guess it's worth a try." Fin sighed.

Roary knelt down to help Fin take his pumpkin off. Jesster and Koal went over to help Mo. Jax just watched resentfully, rubbing his chest where Kan had hit him. Kan hit hard.

Are you afraid? thought Mo to her brother.

I'm so afraid. Fin trembled. *What if I don't want to remember?*

Too late now, thought Kan.

Roary pushed up and backward. Jess and Koal shoved forward and down. The pumpkins came free with a wet squelch.

Kan looked into his friends' faces for the first time.

He started to scream.

CHAPTER NINE

MONSTERS

Kan screamed into their minds. And apologized. And screamed. And apologized.

But, despite the noise, Fin and Mo couldn't stop staring at *each other.*

"You have brown hair!" Mo said.

"You have black hair!" Fin said.

"You have *hair,*" they both said.

"Yeah? Well, *you're* wearing clothes!" Fin accused.

"So are you!" Mo shot back.

AHHHHHH! screamed Kan.

"You have blue eyes, Fin. They're *horrible!*" she giggled with delight. "But they're nice, too. But horrible. But nice."

"You have green ones. They're . . . they're just nice."

Green eyes he'd seen before. All his life. He was used to green eyes. Green and black. It was okay. He could get past it. Even if his twin suddenly had brownish-tan skin and eyebrows and other unsettling things, like a chin.

"Do you remember anything?" Roary asked.

"No," Mo said slowly. "I'm the same Mo I've always been. I'm an enderman."

"You, Fin?"

Fin shook his head. "Same old ender-me."

How could this be happening? How could it be real? How could he not remember being human? Fin was an enderman. He *was*. He had to be. What did anything even *mean* if he wasn't? And another, smaller part of him wondered: Was this why they weren't allowed to go to the Enderdome? Was this why everyone left them to live alone on an old boat? Did everyone, somehow, somewhere deep down, know they were *wrong* all along?

AHHHHHH!

Will you stop that? thought Fin. *If anyone should be screaming, it's us.*

I cannot help it! You are monsters.

No, we're not. We're your friends. Like always. Nothing's different.

Everything is different! To me, you are monsters! Humans! *With hair and skin and big awful EARS.*

But look. Kan, look. She has green eyes. Like you. It's not so bad, is it? She's not so bad. I'm not so bad. Are we?

Mo tried to reach for Kan. Loathsome the zombie pony pawed at her to keep both hands right where they were. *Doesn't the Great Chaos love all surprises?* she thought hopefully.

Not this one, Kan thought. His heart was broken. He couldn't even look at them. *Not this one.*

And then Kan vanished. One minute he was there, the next he was gone.

Kan never did that. Not ever. Just teleported without a word. Without a single thought. Run away from them. Endermen didn't do that. Friends didn't, either.

"This is *so cool*," Roary said. She walked in a little circle around them, checking them out like they were some kind of science experiment. "Maybe it's a spell or a potion. Maybe someone did this to you. Because this isn't how pumpkins work."

"You just said you didn't know how pumpkins worked," Mo pointed out.

"Well, maybe I don't know the exact mechanism, but I know they don't erase who you are when you put them on your head. I've worn one for days at a time and I still know my name is Roary and I like puzzles and exploring diverse biomes and hanging out with my friends and setting things on fire and suspicious stew."

"Yeah, you like it so much you went blind for a week the last time you had your favorite dinner."

"But the time before that I got Fire Resistance for a month! You never know what you're going to get with suspicious stew! I like surprises. *Anyway*, that's not the point; the point is, I might not know the deepest secrets of pumpkin nature, but I know putting one on your head doesn't cause amnesia. So it has to be something else. And I *have* to know what that something else is. Sorry, I'm on your case. And I won't give up till I solve it."

"Could have just hit their heads or something." Koal shrugged. "It doesn't have to be magic."

"Maybe the endermen did it. Maybe they kidnapped you when you were babies!" Roary's voice was breathy with the excitement of a real, honest-to-everything *mystery*.

Fin rubbed his head. All that hair was itchy. He'd never itched like that before. He hated it. "Maybe it's the End itself," he said. "The endermen didn't build all these cities, you know. They don't know who did, either. No one can remember. Maybe if you stay here too long, it does something weird to your memory."

Jesster, Koal, and Roary turned to stare at Fin. He flushed. He'd said something interesting! They were interested in him! And he found that he *wanted* them to think he was clever. Clever and useful. Especially Jess. If these really were his people, if he really was a human, maybe they wouldn't keep him out of whatever they had in place of an Enderdome. If he was good enough, maybe he could belong somewhere. Maybe he could sit next to Jess in the Humandome and train for human battles against various menaces. Maybe he could be so much like a regular human that no one would guess he was brand new at it.

Mo frowned. "But Kan remembers us. He remembers as far back as we do. The Endermas when we were five. All the times he came to the ship when his secondary hubunit chased him out."

"You remember all the way back to when you were five?" said Roary.

"Yes," the twins answered.

"Any further back?"

"Well . . . not much, but isn't that normal? Do you remember a lot of things from before you were five?"

"I guess that's fair," said Jess.

"Okay, but you're just saying 'five,'" Roary pointed out. "Do you mean five years old? Or when you'd been here for five years? Or five months? Or five days?"

"Five years old! Obviously! What kind of a question is that?"

"Do you know that? For *sure*?"

Neither of them could answer. They *wanted* to be sure, but ten minutes ago they'd been sure they were endermen and humans were evil monsters.

Roary started pacing back and forth across the hold of the ship. "See, I don't think you know anything. Maybe it's all connected. The weird endermen making armies and commanders and your friend's green eyes and your memories and all of it. And has anybody else noticed that the end rods have been getting steadily dimmer since we've been standing here? Something really bizarre is going on down here, and we have to rethink *everything*. You two have been living down here with endermen for so long you don't know which way is up. Endermen are monsters, you guys. Do you understand that? They steal and they kill and they hunt. They ruin everything. They're hideous—"

"No, they're not!" Mo cried out.

Loathsome began to chew lightly on her sleeve. The foul foal was almost the size of a bicycle now. Mo wondered when she would stop growing.

"Whatever you say. The point is, endermen are bad. They are capable of anything. They could have done so many terrible things to you to make you believe you were one of them! I can think of like nine or ten without any effort, and I'm a nice person! But what I can't think of is *why*. Why would they convince two humans that they're endermen? What's the point? What's the *plan*?"

"Endermen aren't bad!" Fin protested.

I hate endermen, Grumpo agreed. *They are bad*.

You hate everything, Mo thought. *So what does that prove?*

Just because Grumpo hates everything doesn't mean everything isn't terrible, Grumpo reasoned. *Endermen are terrible. You are terrible. Your twin is terrible. The End is terrible. Burn it all, dragon first.*

Good talk, Grumpo, thought Fin.

Grumpo doesn't talk to humans. The Shulker sniffed. *Humans are terrible.*

"But you met Kan," he said to the humans, who were again looking annoyed with the obvious telepathy going on. "He's not evil."

"Seemed like a pretty normal enderman when he came at me," coughed Jax, rubbing his chest where Kan had hit him.

Koal rolled his eyes. "Oooh, one enderman can cry about how hard his life is. Big deal. Other than Kan, are they even nice to you around here? Are they friendly? Invite you to all the hot ender parties?"

"Not . . . not exactly," said Mo. "We don't have an End, so . . ."

"A what?" interrupted Jax.

"An End. It's like . . . an enderman family. A group of endermen is called an End."

"Super creative," Jax snorted. "And it's called a haunting, by the way. Not an End."

"What? That's horrible." Fin frowned.

"You don't get to say what we call ourselves," Mo snapped.

Koal rolled his eyes. "Well, you're not an enderman, so you don't get to say either."

"Well, we don't have one either way," Fin replied, "so that makes the endermen uncomfortable around us. It's fine, it's not their fault."

Jax looked around. His eyes were calculating. He was working through a big thought. "Hey," he said, squatting down in front of Fin and Mo in a friendly manner. "Where's all your stuff?"

"What stuff?" Fin said defensively.

"You two live here, right? It's a big ship. And if I know anything about endermen I know they love stealing things. So where's all your stuff?"

Mo looked down, her cheeks burning. "They took it," she whispered.

"Who? The nice endermen? The not-bad-at-all endermen? Cleaned you out? You don't even have a scrap to eat or a knife to protect yourself with. Those wonderful, kind, generous endermen didn't even leave you that?"

"Only enough to fight you," Fin mumbled. But he still smarted. He was still angry that Kraj and his goons had robbed them. He was still hungry. Jax was right, but Fin wouldn't give him the satisfaction.

"Well, *clearly* it was worth it. We are soundly defeated, aren't we, guys?"

"Maybe we should take them up to the Overworld," Jess said suddenly. "Sooner rather than later. Maybe they'd recognize something. We could try healing potions. I've got *heaps* of potions at my house. So does Jax. And you never know, maybe someone would recognize them."

"Aw, come on, Jax and me and Roary wanna kill a dragon," Koal said. "That's what we came here for. We can worry about them once we've got the old lizard dead between the eyes. No one's going anywhere until we do, anyway. The exit portal won't appear until that big boy bites it."

"No, you won't touch ED!" screeched Mo. Loathsome screeched with her. "And we're not going to the Overworld either!"

"Our hubunits . . . our . . . our parents *died* there. You can't. It can rain anytime up there. Rain is death . . ." Every enderman knew that. To get caught in the rain was suicide.

"No, they didn't," Roary said, exasperated. "I don't know who your parents were, but they were definitely human! Humans are fine with rain! Promise!"

"I don't want to go to the Overworld!" Mo clung to her baby horse. Fluid oozed down Loathsome's neck. "Fin, don't let them take us. We don't belong there."

"For god's sake, do you even really know that you're twins?" Jesster threw up her hands.

"Of COURSE we're twins," they yelled together.

"You don't look anything alike. What evidence do you have that you're even related at all? Aren't you curious? Isn't any chance of getting your memory back worth it? It's really nice out there, you know. It is. You'll love sunshine. Everyone loves sunshine."

"Well, I *don't*!" Fin snarled. Once, he'd dreamed about going to the Overworld. Avenging his hubunits. Serving the Great Chaos. But it was too much, too fast. All he wanted in this moment was to stay on his ship with his twin and his shulker where it was safe and familiar and solid beneath his feet. He couldn't think like this. He needed to talk to Mo and work it all out in his own good head. He didn't need a bunch of monsters yelling at him. (But were they monsters? If they were, what was he?)

The endermen should have let him go to the Enderdome. Maybe he would have learned something that would have provided a clue to all this.

Mo backed up against the hull of their end ship. "It's *not* nice up there. It's the Land of Order, a miserable wasteland where the wicked rule! It's poison and death! I won't go, I won't. And if you think you're going to sail out of here and murder ED, you've got another think coming. You won't leave this ship. This is *our* territory. *You're* trespassing. And pretty soon the others are going to realize you're here after all and they'll come. You'll find out where our stuff went and you won't like it." *But we won't like it either*, Mo thought to herself. *We're human. We're them. The End won't know us. They'll cut us down without a single tear.* "I don't care how many others have come with you. I don't care how big your army is. You're invaders and the End is plenty strong enough to destroy you."

"What others? It's just us," Koal said, confused. "What are we meant to be invading again?"

I hate you all, Grumpo thought passionately. *Grumpo will not be ruled. Grumpo is unruleable!*

Jax stood up straight and clapped his hands together. "Welp," he announced, "I'm bored. This is stupid and I'm bored."

Jax leapt forward, faster than Mo would have thought possible. He grabbed her by the arm, dug into his pocket, and teleported himself, the former enderman, and the zombie horse out of the ship and into the darkness.

Fin blinked after her. His sister was gone and he had no way to follow her.

He was alone for the first time in his life.

Sometimes the player dreamed it was lost in a story.

Sometimes the player dreamed it was other things, in other places. Sometimes these dreams were disturbing. Sometimes very beautiful indeed. Sometimes the player woke from one dream into another, then woke from that into a third.

—Julian Gough, Minecraft "End Poem"

CHAPTER TEN

MAY THE GREAT CHAOS SMILE UPON YOU

Commander Kraj paced back and forth on a pale yellow courtyard above a craggy, forbidding island shore. Captain Tamat and
Corporal Murrum paced with him, a respectful distance behind.
His bodyguard, their ranks swelled from eight to twelve now,
stood gathered round the doorway from the courtyard into a massive tower that soared into the night. Almost a church, you might
say, if you didn't know that it was one.

They waited for their audience with Eresha, the Mouth of the
Great Chaos.

She was late.

Endermen thought of this place only in hushed, awestruck
tones. Terminus, the holy island, where the Grand High and Glorious Cathedral of Entropy lay hidden from all outsiders. Hidden
from most endermen, too, in fact. The Mouths of the Great

Chaos had long ago decided that things seemed holiest when most people couldn't have them. They had chosen this place. There was no good beach to come ashore easily. There were many sharp rockfaces and steep cliffs where you could fall to your death before you even realized you had made the fatal slip. And there was no end ship attached to the huge and gnarly city on the north edge of the island. Everything about Terminus whispered death and secrets. Death, and secrets, and Chaos.

Now, endermen swarmed over every inch of crag, cliff, or stone.

They all came to hear from Eresha. What was going to happen now? Where were the humans? Was it safe to go home? The stress and strain of being so vastly intelligent was beginning to wear on the endernation. They much preferred the relaxation of their own Ends, clever enough to decide what to have for dinner, not quite clever enough for higher math.

Eresha, the Mouth of the Great Chaos, had not yet emerged from her residence.

Commander Kraj could see her in her window. Her dark shape behind the banners. The old witch kept him waiting on purpose, he just *knew* it. But Kraj was not just a dotty old enderman no one wanted to listen to. Not anymore. He was somebody now. He was a commander. Commander meant people *had* to listen.

He sniffed the night air. Kraj hadn't slept since the Endmoot. He couldn't afford it. Sleep was weakness. Sleep was laziness. The commander peered into the crowds below. So far below they seemed like one huge black mass to him up here. And to them, Kraj and Murrum and Tamat and the rest of his bodyguard were as invisible as memory.

Commander Kraj shook his huge, square-jawed head. He could feel his wits dulling. He needed more.

Kraj sent out his thoughts into the throng. Just two or three would be enough. *Come to the seventh courtyard of the Cathedral of Entropy, my follower,* he called, the touch of his mind caring, calm. *The Great Chaos has important work for you.*

In a quarter of an hour, three young endermen walked uncertainly through the door. They looked around for their important work. The work given to them specially by the divine source of the universe.

Commander Kraj smiled. His mouth was little more than a tear in his face, but in the endless space of his mind, Kraj's grin was as vast as a mountain range. He could feel strength flow through him as their intelligence stacked with the others' and his own. *Ahhhh,* he thought. *Yes. That is better. That is correct.*

Kraj, my fragment. Another mind cut through his own like a ship through water.

Eresha.

How dare she? Kraj was no one's fragment. He was a cruxunit. Long before Eresha replicated from the hubunit stem, Kraj was whole and undivided, walking the primeval world like a giant. Perhaps having fragments at all had been a mistake. Eresha should have been grateful to him, and to the other cruxunits who survived the eons, wherever they were. If not for them, where would the End be now?

The Mouth took in all of them. Kraj, his subordinates, the platoon that served as his own private brain bank. But not so private as all that. Eresha stood taller and thought more clearly in the presence of so many strong endermen, too. Kraj would have liked to hoard their power for himself. But it didn't work that way.

He couldn't keep his mind sharp and Eresha's dull just to get his way. Ender intellect only multiplied in groups. It could not divide.

Thank you for your gracious patience, the Mouth thought.

Kraj considered that never again would the endermen be this wise and calm. Never again would they come together like this. So many of them. So many. Why had they never done this before? Why did they not *always* stay together like this, and conquer all the worlds above and below?

Eresha was not really an old witch. She was younger by far than Kraj. No cracks spoiled her beautiful dark face. No limp slowed her down. Kraj remembered the day Eresha became the Mouth of Chaos. An Endermas long gone by, when he was young enough to imagine the seat might be his instead of some young enderman's.

We await your orders, Your Excellency, Mouth of Chaos, bowed Kraj.

He didn't mean that obedient bow or those obedient words. Eresha knew it. Kraj knew it. They each knew what the other knew. Telepathy made diplomacy so difficult, hardly any enderman bothered with it.

I have no orders for you, spawn of misrule, the Mouth thought, dipping her head to accept his submission.

What do you mean?

Eresha began her own pacing.

The war is over. More precisely, there is no war. There are no humans here. It is over. It was a mistake.

Kraj stared at her.

Are you not relieved? she thought. *No death, no bloodshed, no horror of loss. Go home to your End. All of us will go home to our*

Ends. We will live in peace again. Return the weapons and armor and supplies to the fragments on the end ship. We will not need them. We need only one another once more. I have communed with the Great Chaos. This is the path of the endermen.

You are a fool, Commander Kraj thought harshly.

You may not speak to me that way, fragment, Eresha barked in his mind.

I am not a fragment. I am older than you. And it seems I am far more intelligent. Only a fool would believe that since we cannot see the enemy today, there is no enemy at all. I tell you, the humans would not just give up. The End is rich and beautiful and vast. What general leading the human horde would simply walk away from such spoils? What knights would prepare themselves for battle and then wander off before the plunder? They are coming, Eresha. They are already here. Just because the mutant greenboy is not a double agent and saboteur does not mean there are none. How can you be so dense?

The Mouth stood very still, controlling her anger in a way no enderman could unless the whole teeming nation of them stood shoulder to shoulder. Perhaps she was stronger than Kraj thought. The crowds below were too far away to have an effect. They were on equal footing. Yet she could keep her temper easily. Kraj could barely stop himself from boiling over.

I have communed with the Great Chaos. This is the path of the endermen. I have spoken, she thought icily.

You have spoken wrongly, snapped Kraj.

Captain Tamat and Corporal Murrum stepped away from their commander in horror. The Mouth could not be wrong. It was impossible. She alone had the ear of the Great Chaos. She could not even be questioned. They stepped away to avoid the lightning bolt or fireball that would surely obliterate Kraj where he stood.

Nothing happened to him.

And what is this enemy you speak of, Kraj? Eresha thought. Her magenta eyes filled with impatience and contempt. She thought he was so far beneath her. Kraj fumed. *Humans? We see humans every day in the Overworld. It is very little trouble to kill one if they irritate you. If you want to find your enemy, it is as simple as finding a house and waiting for them to return to it. Why wash our country in ender blood when, and I cannot stress this enough, nothing is happening and no one is here?*

Yes, humans! The commander exploded. *Of COURSE they are our enemies! Anyone who is not of the End is our enemy. Anyone who is not like us! Anyone outside our great End! They kill us for sport. They steal our hearts to travel just a little faster. They gouge out our eyes to decorate their doorways to our country, where they do nothing but pillage and murder. The End is for endermen!* he thundered.

But it is not, Eresha continued calmly. *You forget yourself. You forget your Enderdome training. It is also for shulkers, for endermites, for chorus trees and the ender dragon itself. Every country is shared among many. And once, the End was for whoever built these great towers and palaces and pillars and roads. For we certainly did not. Some ancestor of ours took it from them, whoever they were. This is the path of the Great Chaos, my fragment. It is not always kind.*

I do not want to be like them. Do you, Eresha? How many times have humans come to the End and cut a path of dead endermen and stolen treasure throughout our world?

Many, Eresha admitted. *I cannot count them all.*

Do you remember your first invasion?

The Mouth of the Great Chaos nodded. *I was a fragment. First of my End. Little cleverer than a bright wolf, even with all my family gathered, for then there were only three of us. Three of us, and two of them. Two were enough. I had never seen anything like it. One seemed to command the very elements. When she killed us, we were powerless to stop her. Frozen in time or burning to death when no fire was nearby. She was like water itself. Like rain. She fell on us and we died. Endermen feared her, but marched on. That is who we are. And wherever he walked, fire followed him. They took everything. It was years before my End recovered. Sometimes, I think it never did.*

Kraj threw up his arms. *Then you know I am right! They must be stopped! You were right before. Why wash our country in blood? We should take theirs! Together, we could march on the Overworld and destroy all their works. Wipe out the Forces of Order once and for all. Together, endermen are unstoppable. It is only because we insist on staying apart like stunted donkeys that we do not rule this universe. Perhaps we should change. Evolve. Perhaps there should be a new law: No enderman shall henceforward ever be alone.*

Eresha rolled her eyes at his little speech. *I also remember rising up to the Overworld and slaughtering a village of humans because I and my fellow-fragments simply wished to do it. This is the balance of the Great Chaos and the Forces of Order. I accept it. I suggest you do, too. There is no threat. Go home. You are no longer a commander, but simply Kraj again. Go home to your fragments and sub-fragments and sub-sub-fragments. I have spoken.*

No. No. Kraj's blood thickened and ran cold. She took his title. He felt it as painfully as a blow from a sword. She couldn't do that. She couldn't rob him like that. She couldn't make him go back to no one listening to him. To everyone laughing at batty old Kraj and paying him no attention. He wouldn't let her.

Telepathy made diplomacy very difficult, it was true. Betrayal was even harder. You couldn't think about it for even an instant before you did it. You had to act faster than the speed of thought. Faster than your brain telling your arms to move.

Just that fast, Kraj lifted Eresha, the Mouth of the Great Chaos, off her feet and flung her off the edge of the seventh courtyard of the Grand High and Glorious Cathedral of Entropy. She plummeted silently into nothingness. Black into black. Enderman into the End.

Kraj, commander once more, stood and watched her fall. He was filled with the most extraordinary calm. And why stop at commander, now that he thought of it? Why stop at all?

All hail the Great Chaos, he thought after her.

CHAPTER ELEVEN

THE HEART OF AN ENDERMAN

Jax materialized on a sandy yellow outcropping of rock. The void yawned away beneath. His toes skittered on the edge, sending pebbles tumbling over and down into nothing. Mo and Loathsome popped into space next to him, fury in her eyes, excitement and interest in the horse's.

"What did you do?" Mo hissed.

"Cut through the crap and made a command decision," Jax said, rolling his eyes. He pointed behind them.

A thunderous roar echoed somewhere far above them. ED was flying in its long, slow circles in the distance. Jax had brought them close to the dragon's island. But why?

And Jax teleported! That could only mean he had an ender pearl. He was packing the absolute soul of some poor dead enderman somewhere. Where? And who was it? Mo didn't suppose she'd ever know the answer to the second question.

"Shall we? After you, my lady," Jax said with a mock bow.

"Shall we what?"

Jax glanced up. "Well, you can stay here while I go up and make quick work of that dragon so we can get out of here and figure out what's up with your whole—" He gestured at Mo, Loathsome, either or both. "—situation. Or, since you and your pet lizard are so cuddly and close, you could come up with me and distract him so I can try to one-shot the old monster and then we can head up to the Overworld as friends who had a fun adventure together killing interesting things. I'd rather the second. I'm not awful like you said. I'm really not. I'm just . . . ambitious and highly motivated by insurmountable challenges. That's what my hubunit used to say, anyway." He winked at her.

"Why do you even care about me or my twin or what happened to us?"

"Oh, I don't," Jax assured her. "I just want to figure it out before Roary does. Can you win at solving mysteries? Because I want to win at solving mysteries. I just want to win full stop. It's kind of my thing."

Mo glared at Jax. "I'm not helping you kill my friend. And I'm not going anywhere with you. I hate you. You had no right to teleport me without my permission. You had no right to *touch* me without my permission—"

"Is he your friend though?" Jax interrupted.

"It's not a him!"

"Whatever!"

"You know I can just teleport away, right?" Mo yelled. "I don't have to stay here with you at all."

Jax crossed his arms. "Go ahead. See, I don't think you can. I think you're not in your enderman suit anymore. I think you can't do anything I can't do, and I don't think you have the ender pearls to do it."

Mo froze. Was it true? Was she stuck moving from place to place on her slow, heavy legs like any other human girl? She hesitated. She knew she should just do it, do it right now, blink out here and blink on somewhere else. But what if it didn't work? What if Jax was right? Mo didn't think she could bear it if he was.

Loathsome gave a low, nervous whinny. Something moved in the distance. Something out on one of the other crags on the underside of the ender dragon's island. Something almost the same color as the great sky beyond.

An enderman was standing out there on the rocks. Probing the air with her long, black fingers.

Mo was so excited she forgot nearly everything that had happened to her over the past two hours. She forgot that no endermen were roaming around on ED's island as they usually would, keeping one another calm and clever. She forgot that nearly everyone had answered Kraj and Eresha's call to arms. She called out to the enderman with her mind, waving her arms in the air.

Hello! All hail the Great Chaos! Help! Help me! I've been kidnapped by this human! He's going to attack ED! Help us! Where is your End? I am Mo, twin of Fin. Do you know me?

The enderman turned toward Mo. It was wearing one of the golden chestplates Fin and Mo had collected and Kraj had commandeered. The metal glinted in the dim End light. The enderman's purple eyes narrowed. Its skin flushed red with rage. It screamed a scream of total hate and eternal fury into the sky. Its thoughts were not elegant. They were not organized into tidy sentences. There was only one enderman, after all. One enderman alone is nothing but the shape anger takes when it wants to walk the world.

DIEDIEDIEDIEDIEDIE

It charged her.

As it crossed the distance between them, Mo recognized the enderman.

No, she thought. *Lopp, no, it's me!*

The enderman did not stop.

Lopp, stop! Remember when you offered to be my hubunit? A unit of superior strength and power? Now would be a great time! Lopp, come on! It's me! It's still just me!

But it wasn't Lopp, not really. Not out here, by herself, with no one else around. There was nothing in her mind for Mo to latch on to. There was no *her* there.

Lopp's fist collided with Mo's face. Loathsome reared up to protect her mother, spraying black and yellow fluid from her churning muscles.

"Idiot!" Jax yelled, stomping toward them. "You don't *call* to them, for frick's sake."

Lopp landed a blow between Mo's shoulder blades. She went flying and sprawled on the yellow rock. The enderman hurled herself at Jax and got a hit in against his ribs. He grunted, but that was all.

"It's just one mob, geez," Jax huffed. "You can't handle one mob by yourself?"

"I don't want to handle her!" Mo shoved back at Lopp's rampaging form. She tried to be gentle. It wasn't easy to shove someone around a cliff that dropped off into infinite space without hurting them. Much harder than just punching them until they fell off the edge. Lopp's dark body flushed where Mo hit her. It seemed to only make her angrier.

Lopp, it's me! It's Mo! I know I look different, but I'm not different! Same old Mo! I'm just a fragment, I'm no danger to you. Take me away from him, we can go find Kraj's army together.

Lopp swung her arms wildly, thoughtlessly. One fist caught Loathsome under the chin and slammed her into the rock wall. The other smashed Jax's nose.

Yes! Get him! Try not to get my horse though. She's going to come with us.

Lopp screeched and lifted Mo up off her feet by her throat.

Wait, no! Mo thought frantically. *That's not what I meant. Please, Lopp. You must remember me. I need a hubunit of superior strength!*

But all the enderman saw was a human girl. An enemy. A monster.

Jax pulled an iron sword out of his pocket. (How did he fit so much in there?) Without thinking about it much at all, he stabbed Lopp through the chest.

No! Mo thought.

"No!" she screamed.

Loathsome gurgled furiously and sank her sharp teeth into the enderman's arm. Jax put one foot up against the sagging, dying enderman to push her off the blade of his sword. Lopp's magenta eyes blazed hate and pain. Her fist tightened on Mo's throat.

DIE, the thing that used to be Lopp thought.

And then, faster than a breath, there was no one at all standing on the outcropping of yellow rock. No girl, no boy, no battle.

The ender dragon howled somewhere far above.

CHAPTER TWELVE

THE OVERWORLD

Space flipped upside down. The black sky and yellow rock suddenly floated above them. Then they flipped inside out. Then a brilliant light obliterated the world around them. It consumed the End and the island and the crag of rock and the rumbling of ED in one huge white flash.

When the flash faded, Mo was standing on green grass. Jax pulled his sword out of Lopp and stumbled backward a little, catching his balance. Loathsome bit down harder. She growled with her mouth full of enderman. But it didn't matter. Lopp was already dying. She'd tried to teleport away, but all it had done was drag them all with her into the Overworld. The enderman crumpled to the ground. Her eyes faded as she fell. Mo reached out after her, but Lopp was gone. Mo's green, human eyes filled with tears.

"What were you doing out there all alone, you dummy?" she whispered. "You died! You didn't have to. Only dummies die."

"Did we just teleport out of the End completely, like, for real? Neat!" said Jax. He looked down at the loot on the ground. "Cool chestplate." He put his hands on his hips and sighed heavily. "I'm gonna have to find another portal. So annoying. Doing things twice is stupid."

Mo blinked. She hadn't even noticed that they'd teleported. They'd teleported, and she was somewhere else. Somewhere *very* else.

The sky above Mo shone deep, royal blue. A jungle of trees surrounded her, stretching on as far as she could see. Little red flowers bobbed here and there. Brown mountains rose up in the distance. A few yards away, a bright blue lake sparkled in the golden sunshine. As she watched, dumbfounded, a huge black squid splashed its tentacles out of the water, then slammed them back down, sending up a spray of white foam. It was as though the squid had waved at her, welcoming her to the world.

A single, fat, round-cheeked pig stared at them, its mouth hanging open in shock.

"Oh," Mo said softly. "They're pink after all. Kan always said. I never believed it. But they are. So pink." She reached out her hand to pet the pig.

The pig did not want to be petted. The pig was much more concerned about Loathsome at the moment. Its black eyes slid over the horse, trying to make sense of it. The two animals gazed at each other for a moment. A glob of lung fluid swelled up on Loathsome's chest and, with a massive PLOP, dripped onto the ground.

The pig bolted away.

After a few moments, Loathsome began to nibble lightly on the dead enderman's head. *Brains?* she said hopefully. Like most babies, once the pony had a new idea in her head, she wouldn't be letting it go anytime soon.

But before Mo could teach her horse about eating friends' brains, Lopp disappeared in a curl of smoke. Ender bodies didn't last long. The Great Chaos hates waste. When she'd disappeared, her pearl remained. And the chestplate.

Jax nudged the armor with his toe. "I've never seen an enderman wearing human gear before. Ever." He glanced shrewdly at Mo. "Is this yours?"

"Yeah," Mo said, part of her still so angry that her people had robbed her. And here was Lopp, not fighting in an apocalyptic war of all against all but wearing her stuff like she'd just borrowed a shirt.

He handed it back to her. The metal was warm in the sunshine. Mo gathered it to her like a long-lost teddy bear. She held it tight. It smelled like home. Just a little bit like the End. Like her ship and her brother and her good old life.

"Thank you," she whispered.

"You don't have to thank me," Jax said quietly. For the first time, his voice sounded very serious and gentle. "It's your loot. No one should have taken it from you in the first place."

How Orderly of him, Mo thought. But she was so grateful. To have one piece of her collection back. One piece of *herself* back. Mo fastened it on. It felt good and solid and *real*.

Jax bent down, picked up the ender pearl lying on the ground, turned around, and started walking again.

"Whoa! Wait! Don't you dare," yelled Mo. "You give that to me!"

"No way, I made the kill, I get the drop. That's your loot, this is mine. I'm being *really* fair here."

"But it's *her* pearl! That would be like me taking your brain for a souvenir."

Brains? piped up Loathsome.

No, Mo snapped back.

"She had a name, Jax. Do you know her name? Because I do. You have no right to it. Give it here. I'll take it home. I'll take care of it. It's mine."

"I mean, it's *not* yours. You aren't an enderman. You're not one of them. You seem to be having a lot of trouble with that. I have a lot more right to it than you. And no, I don't want to know her name, that's fricking creepy. All ender pearls look the same and are the same and I like it like that. Look at it this way, if you kill something, doesn't it honor that thing to use all its parts and not let anything go to waste? I honor the strength and power of your weird monster friend. So I will make sure to honor what is left of her by using it in strength and power." But Jax saw the look on Mo's face and knew she wouldn't let it go. "Fine, whatever, take it. I have tons of them. I don't care."

Jax tossed the pearl behind him. Mo scrambled in the grass for it. It was still warm. Poor Lopp. She couldn't stop wondering why Lopp had been so far from Telos. Wasn't everyone still preparing for war? No one knew the "war" was just four kids raiding for loot. It had to be something simple. Something she just wasn't seeing. One enderman alone couldn't hold on to a complicated thought.

Mo squinted. Her eyes burned. She'd never seen sunlight. She didn't know *how* to see it without hurting. It was just so *bright*. How could anyone stand it? That big burning ball of flame hanging over them *all the time*? And all those colors! (Blue for Fin's eyes; green for hers.) They throbbed. So vivid and loud! Nothing like the soothing violet and soft yellow and comforting black of the End. Nothing like anything Mo had ever known.

"Anything look familiar?" Jax asked. His voice was almost . . . nice.

Mo tried. She really tried. "No," she gave up. "I've never seen anything like this place. What is *that*?"

Jax glanced around. "Pretty standard forest biome," he said.

"No, I mean that." Mo pointed up. She couldn't imagine what to call it. It was so big and heavy-looking. So alien.

"That?" Jax followed her eyes. Then he looked back at Mo. Then up again. "That is a cloud," he finished, shaking his head. "Koal was right. Wow. Just *wow*."

Loathsome stood up on wobbly, half-rotted legs. She nibbled experimentally at the grass. She swallowed. The grass slid down her throat and fell out of a hole in her stomach where her ribs showed through.

"This way," said Jax, walking off to the north. He walked with easy purpose and familiarity. This was his place.

"Where are we going?" Mo asked, paralyzed with fear. "Do you think it'll rain?"

But it didn't matter, did it? It didn't matter if it rained. Because Mo was not an enderman. The rain couldn't hurt her. She tried to think. She tried to remember. Tried to remember a time before the End. Tried to remember *anything* other than the End. Tried to remember a time when her life was green and blue and brown. When her life was this world, and not the other. But there was nothing there. Nothing. All she could remember was Fin and Kan and ED and the long night of her home. This was all so *impossible*.

Mo looked at her horse. Loathsome seemed to have stopped growing, for the moment. She was big enough to ride, if you didn't mind the mess. *You still like me, don't you?* she said to the undead pony. *You don't mind whether I'm human or enderman.*

The pony turned and nuzzled her shoulder. It was a very wet, cold nuzzle. Then it was a sharp nuzzle.

Hey! No biting.

Loathsome looked confused. As she was growing older, she was beginning to understand some things about life as a zombie horse. *Mumma. Mumma. B . . . B . . . Braaains?* she asked, uncertain.

No, Mo scolded. *Bad horsey. No brains. At least not mine.*

Loathsome pawed the ground glumly. *Braaaains,* she complained.

"You coming?" called Jax behind him.

Mo didn't want to, actually. She did not remotely appreciate being kidnapped out into the Overworld, a place she'd never *really* even wanted to visit, by a jerk who didn't seem to care about much of anything but looting and killing ED. Well, the looting she could understand. But the ED-killing? Mo had to draw a line somewhere. The until-very-recently enderman followed anyway, though. If she lost sight of Jax, she'd never get back. She'd be stuck in this bright, loud, overwhelming place with no one. Mo scrambled up a little hillside after him. Loathsome did not understand why her mother did not simply ride her, preferably toward any fresh local brains. But she was still very new, and accepted such unexplainable choices.

Reluctantly, Mo kept walking. It was the only option.

On the other side of the hill sat Jax's house. It was a very nice house. Honestly, it was an *amazing* house. Almost a castle. It had four towers, twenty windows, and three gargoyles. The walls were all strong grey stone. Mo, Jax, and Loathsome passed under a huge portcullis on the other side of a drawbridge over the little blue moat flowing all the way around the fortress. Torches burned on either side of every door and window. Pretty little patches of wheat and flowers grew around the banks of the moat. Loathsome stuck her oozing nose into the wheat and sniffed.

Mumma! Graaaaains? she neighed, though it was really more of a phlegmy gurgle.

Mo laughed a little. *Sure, baby. All yours.*

The zombie pony kicked up her hind legs in joy. Bone showed through the grey, rotting skin. Her thick, ridged, toenaily hooves glinted dully in the sun. She mowed through a patch of wheat so fast Jax couldn't shoo her off his landscaping in time.

"Ugh," he said helplessly as the pony started on his flowers. "Can you not . . . *leak* on my garden?"

But Mo didn't seem to care about the murky spinal fluid beading up and dribbling off of Loathsome's body onto his lawn.

"Come on," Jax sighed, resigned to losing his front yard entirely. "The sun's going down. You don't want to be caught outside at night. Trust me."

They left the horse to her first feast and started over the bridge.

Mo jogged a little to keep up. "You're so lucky you found this place! If I were you I'd never leave it! You never know who might try to take it while you're gone."

"Well, first of all, I didn't find it, I built it."

"All by yourself?"

Jax straightened up a bit, quite proud. "All by myself. Took ages. Even designed the gargoyles. But really, it's not that good. There're way bigger castles and stuff farther inland. Some of them are even mine! I was just figuring things out when I built this. I've done way better ones since. But this one's my favorite, because it was my first."

"I didn't realize you built things. I thought you just killed them." Maybe Jax wasn't really so bad. Anyone who could build something so magnificent couldn't be *that* bad.

Jax waved his hand dismissively. "Oh, I don't really do much building anymore. This is all old stuff, from when I was a kid. I got bored. I was spending all my time fighting off creepers and zombies and chasing them away from my houses. Then I realized *I* could just chase *them*, whenever I wanted, and I didn't need any houses for that at all! Way more exciting. I never get bored anymore. Hey! What are you doing! Stop that!"

Mo snatched her hand back guiltily. Where a moment ago there had been a smooth, unbroken stone wall, there was now a square hole.

"All hail the Great Chaos," whispered Mo.

She'd hardly even known what she was doing before it was done. It had been automatic, like a reflex.

"Sorry!"

"What did you do? What's wrong with you? I just told you how long it took me to build this place."

"I couldn't help it! It's just so beautiful and perfect."

"Yeah, it is! So what the crap?"

"You designed it all so . . . so precisely. It's so complete. So correct. So . . . so *Orderly*."

"SO WHAT? YOU WRECK IT?" Jax looked down at her with disgust. "Of course you do. Because you're an enderman. That's what you do. You see something good and you punch a hole in it."

"I served the Great Chaos," Mo argued, steeling her spine. "You do what humans do—you see something and you kill it!"

"What are you talking about?"

"The universe! Lopp!"

"YOU'RE A CRAZY PERSON!" Jax screamed, and stomped off into the house. The portcullis opened into a long hallway with a lot of heads of various exotic creatures on the walls and, naturally, more torches.

"I made it better!" Mo yelled after him. "Now it's perfect, because it's imperfect!"

"Shut up, mob!" Jax yelled back. "I don't have to listen to crazy people!"

Mo ran down the long hallway to catch up with him. Loathsome ran after her. By the time they got to the boy, both were out of breath. Loathsome because her lungs had been born rotting. Mo because she'd never had to breathe the air of the Overworld before. It was so rich and full her body didn't know what to do with it.

"Jax," she panted. "Listen. I'm not crazy. Well, maybe I am, but not because of this. The universe was created in a battle between the Great Chaos and the Forces of Order. They struggled against each other for eons. Sometimes Chaos prevailed, and made the endermen, and the shulkers, and the creepers, and fire itself. Sometimes Order prevailed, and made humans and sheep and pigs and medicine and stones and trees. Finally, their conflict ended as it always must: in a draw. They looked around and all their creations surrounded them: They had made the universe. So everything serves either the Great Chaos or the Forces of Order, and they will always fight. It's in their nature. I served the Great Chaos. I made your house better. More beautiful. More perfect."

"You made it weaker! Anyone could crawl in through that hole!"

"Yes, yes, exactly! And if someone did, what amazing things might happen? What kind of exciting story might start for you? A dangerous one, even. They're more exciting when they're dangerous. You should never be able to predict what will happen next in life. That's boring. That's the Forces of Order. When Chaos reigns, *everything* is exciting, because *anything* could happen. Every second is a surprise. So you can't get mad at endermen for perfecting your houses and all that, because we're *helping* you, really. When you think about it."

"Okay," said Jax with a little smile, the kind of smile that said he thought he'd won the argument already. "Then you can't be mad at me for killing that enderman back there."

"Oh yes, I can."

"Oh no, you can't. I was just serving the Great Chaos. She definitely couldn't have predicted what happened to her. It was one hundred percent a surprise, I guarantee it. It was a very exciting story."

Mo didn't know what to say to that. It sounded right and wrong at the same time. She didn't want to let Jax be right about anything. But it certainly *had* been chaotic. She decided to change the subject.

"What were you going to do with her pearl?" Mo asked hesitantly.

Jax motioned for her to follow him down another stone hall. This one was much more narrow and less grand. "Teleport," he said. "Maybe grind it up to make another ender chest. Dunno."

"I heard that humans can use pearls to teleport." A thought suddenly occurred to Mo. "Wait a minute," she said, stopping in the middle of the grey cobblestone hallway. "Fin and I have always been able to teleport. And if we aren't endermen, we don't have ender pearls. So how could we do that? We teleported just fine. All day long."

Jax looked her up and down. He squinted one eye.

"I bet I know," he said. "Hold still."

Jax got up close to Mo. She didn't like that at all. She didn't like Jax. She didn't like how he looked or how he talked or how he acted. She didn't like that he'd grabbed her off her ship. The only thing she liked even a little bit about the big human kid was that he'd given her the chestplate back, and been quite nice about it. He seemed to be everything she'd been taught humans were: loud, aggressive, greedy, rude, and eager to take anything he wanted.

You're a human, though, Mo thought to herself. *If humans are those things, so are you. And how else did you get an entire ship full of treasure than by taking what you wanted when you wanted it?*

Jax stuck his hand into Mo's pocket. Pocket! She had pockets! She'd never thought about pockets before. Ever. Endermen don't need them. He scrabbled around in there for a minute, scrunching up his face. His face was so close to hers. She'd never been so close to a human. Except Fin. But she hadn't known Fin was human, had she?

He'd been in there a while. How big could a pocket be? Finally, Jax squared his feet and pulled out, one after the other, a strange pale-gold doll, a black egg, and an ender pearl so old its dust was covered in dust. It looked like a collapsed balloon. As soon as the air hit it, the pearl started falling apart.

Jax and Mo stared at the egg, the doll, and the pearl.

"You have a totem of undying," Jax whispered, stunned. "Where did you get that?"

"How should I know? I didn't know I had pockets till just now. But that stuff is *heavy*. How could I be carrying it and not know?"

The ender pearl bubbled into mush and began to seep down through the floorboards. *There goes teleportation,* Mo thought.

"Pockets," Jax said slowly, his mind clearly working through something else entirely. "It's a human thing. It's not really a pocket, it's a shortcut to an empty block of space-time that can hold whatever you want because it's both infinitely big and infinitely small at the same time. You don't feel the weight or the bulk of your stash. There're limits, but mostly you can carry anything, no problem. You could teleport because you had an ender pearl the whole time. So you're no better than me. That pearl belonged to somebody, too. You probably killed them for it."

"I did not!" cried Mo. "I wouldn't!"

But it was so obvious that Jax didn't really care about the pearl or the totem. He reached out his fingers toward the black egg. He seemed almost afraid to touch it. The loud, obnoxious boy was suddenly *reverent*. Full of awe.

"Are you ok?" Mo asked.

"Sorry," Jax muttered, shaking his head. "Look, I'm sorry, I know you're having a whole identity crisis or whatever, but what the *actual* crap, Mo? Why do you have a dragon egg? *How* do you have a dragon egg?"

"Is that a dragon egg?"

"Is that a dragon egg?" Jax screeched in a high-pitched, mocking tone. "YES, THAT'S A DRAGON EGG, YOU MELON. *Where did you get it?*"

"I DON'T KNOW, YOU . . ." Mo wasn't used to insulting people in human terms. She stumbled. "DOUBLE MELON."

Jax shook his head in disbelief. "You've been lying to me this whole time!"

"No, I haven't!"

"You're so high and mighty! Trying to lecture us on right and wrong, killing and not killing. Making me feel bad about myself. Making me feel like I'm *scum*. And the whole time you were carrying around a dragon egg like it's no big deal. Well, it is a big deal, you *freak*. And it's only a *slightly* bigger deal than having a totem of undying when you're supposed to be this poor little lost orphan with amnesia. There's no way you just *found* those things. No one would ever be so careless as to drop one or leave it lying around. In fact, there's no way that egg should even *exist*. You're not going anywhere until we figure this out. Because there's only one way to get a dragon egg for yourself."

"And what's that?"

Jax frowned. "You have to kill the ender dragon."

CHAPTER THIRTEEN

IT'S COMPLICATED

Jax, Mo, and Loathsome had been gone for no more than a few hours.

Fin couldn't remember ever going so long without seeing his twin. Without knowing she was safe and nearby. Without talking to her. It made him nervous. It made him feel unsteady, like he could just tumble off into the night at any moment. The others seemed to have lost a little interest in him once Jax had taken off with Mo. They had other priorities. The mystery could wait until their friend came back.

In the meantime, they were *very* busy.

The humans were building something.

Roary, Koal, and Jesster all had pairs of soft grey wings attached to their backs. They used them to glide from the ship to a smallish island off the port side where they were working. Fin knew what they were. Elytra. A couple of days ago he'd had dozens of pairs of his own. Now, Roary and Koal had to carry him between them when they flew over to their new base. They didn't need anything from the ship. There wasn't much left there anyway, except the small mountain of enchanted books. But Roary wanted them all to stick together over on the new beachhead. She didn't want to leave Fin alone back there.

Fin watched them make quick work of that little island. It was dizzying. Their hands moved so fast and so cleverly. Fin looked down at his own hands. He didn't think he could ever do anything like that. That confident. That purposeful. That *casual*. They must have had some kind of blueprint for whatever they were building, but they never seemed to need to reference it or argue amongst themselves over where to put the next cornerpiece or anything.

Roary and Jesster attacked the grove of chorus trees at the north end of the island. They hacked them up for the wood before Fin could begin to explain how to make chorus corn from the fruits. Koal got busy carving blocks of end stone, the very stuff of the land in the End, out of a little cliff on the west side. Fin didn't think that would be enough to make anything too impressive. You'd have to mine half the islands in the End to build something as big as Telos. And it looked like that was about the size of their plan. But when they pooled the chorus trees and stone at the building site on a flat meadow in the center of the isle, protected by gentle hills on all sides, it quickly became clear the humans weren't relying on just what they could scavenge here.

Something was wrong with their pockets. They could pull anything out of them. Stones, food, weapons, anything. It was like they were wearing his whole ship, as it had been before Kraj and his goons, and shoveling items out as they needed them. It was magic.

"By the Great Chaos," Fin whispered. No one heard him. They had way too much to do.

Roary had half a wall up before Fin knew what he was looking at. She got up on a rise of rock to work on a doorframe. Jess sat cross-legged on the inner side of the new wall, sawing chorus wood up into furniture. Koal dug down into the island earth for a good foundation and started hauling redstone blocks out of his trousers. It was so ridiculous to look at, yet so terrifying. Could all humans do this? Could Fin do it?

None of them seemed to miss Jax at all.

"Well, of course he's our *friend*," Jess said when Fin asked about it. She didn't bother to look up from the stone wall she was building with breathtaking speed. Her pickaxe was a blur. "But he's got his whole mission and he's very focused on it. I'm not about that life. Neither is Roary."

"I'm a *little* about that life," Koal said.

Roary made a gesture with her thumb and forefinger and a tiny space between them. A *little*. She grinned.

"What life?" Fin asked.

Jess bit the inside of her lip. It made her mouth go all crooked. "You shouldn't worry about your sister or Jax. They'll be back. Any minute."

"That's what you told me when they left," Fin said impatiently. "I know. I'm not worried." He was worried.

"No, I know, it's just that when I tell you about Jax, you're *going* to worry, but you shouldn't. He's not a bad guy."

Fin scratched the back of his head. He couldn't get used to having hair. It wasn't right. It was *unnatural*. "It worries me that you're saying that, because nobody said he was bad, but you're already defending him."

Jesster sighed and put down her tools. "Jax likes killing things."

"That's horrible," Fin said.

Jess shrugged. "Is it, though? What do you eat around here?"

"I dunno," Fin said uncomfortably, even though he did know quite well. "Chorus fruits."

"Right, so you kill things all the time. And that's okay, as far as you see it. As long as it's vegetables. And what about endermites? I bet you stomp them as soon as you see them."

"That's not the same thing. Endermites are nasty little pests. They will bite the black out of you as soon as look at you. They're nothing. They're so stupid they barely know they're alive. They're basically mean, walking meat popsicles. It's not like we eat shulkers. And chorus trees are just plants."

"Plants are alive. It's still killing. And I'd bet, if you could get an endermite to talk, they'd have some words about who is a mean, walking meat popsicle."

"But you can't get an endermite to talk. Believe me, I've tried." *I've been lonelier than you can even think of, in your beautiful blue world up there, where everything you could ever want fits in your pocket,* Fin thought, but didn't say.

Jess laughed. "Sure, but you can't get a pig or a sheep or a creeper to talk, either. Jax just . . . Fin, he wants to be safe. He'd never admit it, but that's all it is, deep down. He wants to be safe. He wants *us* to be safe. And you don't know what it's like up there. What comes for you when the sun goes down. We're all on our own in the Overworld, unless we band together, like the four of us. And nothing up there will hesitate to kill us."

"If it's so normal to kill, then why are you acting like Jax is special?"

Jess picked at the corner of the table she was making. "Look, it's fun to fight, okay?" she said defensively. "If you're good at it. And Jax is good at it. We all are, but he's *really* good. So after a while, nobody wanted to mess with him anymore. Even the endermen avoided him. It just wasn't worth it, I guess. So he started wandering out into whatever distant territory he could find. He'd just keep going and going until something attacked him. He became fascinated with hunting rare creatures . . . unique monsters. He took home souvenirs and hung them in his hall. He's a collector. Everybody's got to have a passion, you know? But he's not a bad guy. He wants to be strong and he wants to be safe. Everyone wants that, don't they?"

Fin remembered why they were here. He didn't like it at all. "How did you meet him?"

"Oh, Jax and me've been friends since forever. But we only met Koal and Roary last summer. Jax likes to hunt and fight. I . . . I like to build. I'm the reason he's got all those houses. I taught him how to make something a little stronger and more interesting than a bed with a roof over it. Before me, he was just making big, dumb, plain wooden cubes with a bed inside. No style at all. No *flair*. I love making something out of nothing. Just a wide green field full of trees and boulders and then—presto! Jess happens to it, and it's a pirate ship or a palace or a racetrack. I look at random stuff and I see civilization. Order out of chaos, you know?"

Fin felt a little sick. "I do know," he said, trying to hide his disgust. Chaos was beautiful and alive. Order was ugly and dead. Every enderman knew that. It was like listening to a demon tell him how wonderful living in fire could be. No, it *wasn't* wonderful. It burned your skin off.

"But even though I like to build stuff," Jess went on, "doesn't mean I don't like a good fight or a good hunt. I met Jax in a beach cave. He was cleaning out the cave spiders so you could spend a minute on that beach without having one jump on your head. Horrible things, cave spiders. Poisonous. I was looking for materials to build a library. A place for all the books I find. You can make glass out of good enough sand, you know. A glass library. I liked the idea of that. Anyway, Jax was about to be spider lunch and I gave him a hand. Almost got our heads handed to us. We were just starting out then. He wasn't that good at . . . well, anything. Neither was I. We're loads better now. We traveled together a lot. It's safer in numbers. And last summer we were out hunting skeletons because wouldn't a whole castle made out of bones be fantastic?"

"I guess?" Fin said. It sounded gruesome.

Jess looked at him like he was crazy. He didn't need telepathy to read that look. It *was* fantastic, her eyes said. How could he not agree?

"Well, we followed a skeleton into this huge, amazing swamp. It just went on forever."

Roary jogged over. She settled down next to the half-built table. "You talking about last summer?"

"Yeah," Jess said. "Fin wants to know how we met."

Roary pulled a cooked apple out of her—apparently cavernous—pocket. She munched on it. "You guys saved us from the witch. It was *awesome*."

Jess shuddered, getting into the spirit of her story. "The swamp was huge and soggy and mucky and full of snakes and birds and the moon and quiet. But there's not much good building material in swamps. Not like orchards or mountains. Not for what I like to make, anyway. We couldn't quite get a good shelter up before dark. And as the sun dipped down out of the sky, she appeared in her little swamp hut all lit up with swamp-gas lights. Have you ever met a witch?"

Fin shook his head. There were so many different kinds of creatures up there. He couldn't imagine it. Everyone down here was the same. He never had to worry about seeing something he didn't understand, like a witch or a skeleton or a cave spider.

"They're like chemists with terrible outlooks on life," Roary piped up. "That's why me and Koal were there. I'm sure Jess told you she's a builder, Jax is a hunter—well, I like crafting. Mixing things up and seeing if they explode or create something totally new and totally useful. It's the best thing in the world. Like solving a mystery, but you don't even know what the mystery *is* while you're solving it. Kind of like you and your sister. So the point is, witches have potions, and potions are great, and I wanted them. You know"—Roary leaned in confidentially—"I think I might chuck it all and become a witch myself someday. I could if I wanted. I'm pretty cranky about most things most of the time, I dig swamps and wearing black and filling up potion bottles with horrible chemicals and horrible magic and horror just generally. If this End thing doesn't work out, it's my backup plan."

By then, Koal had seen them talking and put down his axe to join the group.

"Koal came along because he'd never been to a swamp before," Roary said. Koal nodded.

"I like exploring," he said. "It gets me a little bit of everything—collecting, hunting, crafting, building, or at least looking at buildings. And every once in a while you find gold. Or even diamond ore. A little bit of diamond will keep me happy for a week. But it turns out witches are very selfish and they just want to keep all their magic for themselves. One captured us. She put us in a cell made out of hundreds of poison potions. If we'd tried to escape, we'd have shriveled up and she'd have made people soup out of us. Witches are the worst."

"Well, to be fair, you were going to rob her," Fin said.

"Yeah, but she was gonna *kill* us! That's what I call overreacting. She could always make more potions."

Fin thought about Kraj and his soldiers carting everything he and Mo had ever loved out of their ship and how he'd felt. How angry he'd been. If he'd had hundreds of bottles of poison then, what would he have done?

"Jax and I stormed the place," Jesster picked up the story. "The witch wasn't alone. She had a bunch of creeper friends and a zombie butler. Took us all night to get everyone. Then dissasemble the poison bottle jail and let them out."

"You killed *all* of them?" Fin's face was doing all sorts of things. He'd never had one before, so he didn't know how to just look interested and attentive without showing everything he felt. He frowned, his eyebrows went up and then down again, he grimaced, he squinted, he scratched his head. Their story was ridiculous. All those things he'd never heard of, all those places. They were messing with him. They had to be. Or at least exaggerating. Making themselves sound a lot more dangerous and exciting than any twelve-year-old really could be. Fin and Mo were still just waiting for their lives to start. These humans couldn't really have done all this, could they?

Jess looked uncomfortable. "The zombie butler was already dead . . ." she said with a half-hearted shrug. "Technically."

"She'd have killed all of us if she could. They come out at night. They hunt us. Up there, it's everything in the world against humans. Just surviving is a win. You're so judgmental. Has anyone ever *hunted* you? I didn't think so."

He hadn't ever been hunted, of course he hadn't. But that didn't make it right, did it? A lot of the endermen in the End were tremendously mean, but he didn't kill them. Mo didn't kill them. And yet . . . when the humans talked about the Overworld, the swamp and the witch, the beach cave and the poisonous spiders, the castle made out of bones . . . it all sounded so . . . so *exciting*. So different from the End, where every day was exactly the same, and every night, too. Imagine living in a place where you could never know what might happen next. Imagine living in a place where colors other than yellow, purple, and black existed. In a place where the biggest adventure you could find was something much, *much* more interesting than training in the Enderdome.

"They're just monsters," Koal mumbled. "It's no big deal."

All those visions of the Overworld vanished from Fin's head. "Just monsters? Just *monsters*? Like endermen, you mean?" he shot back, much louder.

Jess rolled her eyes. "Yes, actually, *exactly* like endermen. Endermen are *strange*. They're alien. They're hideous. They're violent and angry even when you're just minding your own business not bothering anyone. But if you commit the high crime of looking at them, as if looking ever hurt anyone, they'll get you. You *have* to get them first. That's all there is to it. Survival of the quickest. Once you've seen an enderman, it's usually too late. They're the worst thing I know about. Do you have any idea how many humans endermen kill up there? Because it is a *lot*. And it's not even like they're doing it to get our loot. When we go down, and regen at our spawn point, we leave everything behind, but they never take it. And let me tell you, respawning is no fun. It hurts like I don't even know what. You're so weak. You can barely move. Everything just *throbs*. Unless you've got medicine on hand and a good friend, or a totem to stop your respawn from happening in the first place, you won't feel like yourself again for a long time."

Fin felt his cheeks burn. "Then what are you doing here? It's nothing but endermen down here! Why couldn't you just leave us alone? You're the monsters, not us. You just show up in our territory and expect to do whatever you want, however you want, with whatever you want, and you don't care if it belongs to you or not. Humans are all the same!"

Koal got red in the face. He was embarrassed. He was angry. He was insulted. "If humans are all the same, you're bad too! You're human, you idiot! And if you had a ship full of loot, I bet a bucket of gold you got it by marching in somewhere, seeing what you wanted, and taking it without asking just like all the other nasty, no-good humans. If your ender-friends knew what you were, they'd treat you the same as they treat us and you wouldn't think they were so great then! Get a grip, Fin, deal with your situation, and face the facts! If humans are monsters, you're a monster, too."

Fin fought desperately not to cry. "According to you, ender-men are the monsters. So I'm one either way!" he screamed. "Just get out! Go away! If you hadn't come I'd still be in my ship with all my stuff and my twin and my best friend and I wouldn't have any problems! I'd still be happy! *What are you doing here?* Why can't you just go back where you came from?"

"It's COMPLICATED!" Roary yelled back. "Just calm *down*. We're just regular people, Fin, just like you."

"Not like me. I never invaded anybody. And Kraj is right. That's what you're doing, even if you're only an army of four. Why do you think you have the right to just show up on someone else's land and start doing and taking whatever you want from whoever you want?"

"That's just how it works in the Overworld," Koal said. "Everybody does it."

"Then the Overworld *sucks*. And so does everybody." Fin crossed his arms over his chest and let out his breath.

"Did you ask before taking every piece of your collection from the place you found it? Even the rocks and the ore and the wood?" Koal fired back. Fin had nothing to say to that. He hated that he didn't.

"It's complicated," he mumbled.

Roary tried to explain. "You want to know why we came? It's not just one thing. We aren't endermen. Every human is completely different from every other human. Yeah, yeah, Jax wants to kill the ender dragon. Big whoop. Lots of people do. It's like how lots of people see a mountain and some of them want to paint it and some of them want to live on it and some of them want to mine it, but most people just *gotta* climb it. So Jax wants to climb it. But we planned to come to the End for a lot of reasons. I wanted to find new materials. I guess that makes me the miner. There's stone and food and treasure down here you can't find anywhere else. Koal wanted to see a place that's pretty much nothing but a legend in the Overworld. He's your painter. Although he was more or less on board with Jax's plan, and so was I."

Koal looked embarrassed. "I like to travel. But once you've got where you're going . . . it's nice to have something to do. I need activities. Or I might as well stay home."

Roary nodded. Fin got the feeling none of them was entirely *off*board with Jax's plan when it came right down to it. "And Jess wanted . . ."

Jesster rubbed her hands on her knees. She could speak very well for herself. "Jess wants to live on the mountain."

"To rule it? With an iron fist? From this castle? Queen of the End?" Fin clenched his fist. *Grumpo will not be ruled. Grumpo is unruleable. And so is Fin.*

Jesster boggled. "No. Just live here. Who wants to rule? What a lot of work. *Jess* got tired of running from all those sweet, nice monsters who definitely didn't want to kill her or knock down everything she ever built. *Jess* thought if she stocked up enough pumpkins, she could build her own little city and live down here and not have to worry about witches or spiders or skeletons or zombie butlers or creepers or anything. She could just build her library of glass and be happy. *Jess* . . . kind of wants to be *you* when she grows up."

Fin looked at Jess with astonishment. *She* wanted to be like *him*? But . . . Jess was strong and confident. She had everything. She was pretty. Soft brown skin and brown hair in a long ponytail and brown eyes. A friendly set to her chin. Not scary. Not flashing with rage. Not a monster. Just a girl who wanted to build a library. He knew another girl like that. His sister. And when his sister came back, if they were going to figure out what had happened to him, it would be this girl and her friends who would help them, not the endermen. Not now. Not once they saw the twins as they really were. Not Kraj or Lopp or Koneka or Eresha the Mouth of the Great Chaos. Maybe Kan. Maybe. But he couldn't count on that and neither could Mo. If he was going to get help, Fin knew he needed to stop calling them monsters. Whether it was true or not.

Fin dried his eyes and took a deep breath. "Building libraries isn't so bad," he sniffed. He smiled shyly. "I even know where you can find some books."

"Really?" Jess said. Her eyes got big and round. "I could have them?"

Fin nodded. "If Mo says it's okay. She will. But it's nice to ask."

"It would only take a couple of trips to ferry them all over here," Roary said. "What's in all those books anyway?"

Fin shrugged. "I don't know. They're enchanted. I've never been able to get one to open."

CHAPTER FOURTEEN

IN THE ARMY NOW

Go on, thought Commander Kraj. *Take it. It will make you stronger.*

The enderfrag Koneka reached out one skinny arm toward the strange, alien thing. She hesitated, uncertain. She looked dark and calm against the glowing Enderdome courtyard. Almost like a grown-up.

All the other enderfrags in the Enderdome watched her carefully. They waited to see what she would do. Everyone liked Koneka. Some endermen were never alone because they were afraid to lose their minds. Koneka was never alone because the other young fragments just felt better about being alive when she was around. Kraj was big and frightening and angry. He had sailed in like a furious black boat with fifteen other endermen who all had funny titles like "Captain" or "Corporal" or "Sergeant" stuck on their names. He had interrupted Left-Hand Human-Punching practice. He had demanded all the frags gather in one place to listen to him. He had commanded Taskmaster Owari not to interfere or interrupt. Commander Kraj made them all want to teleport far away. But Koneka hadn't, so they hadn't. Whatever Koneka did now, they would all do.

What is it? Koneka thought.

You know what it is, fragment, Kraj scoffed. *Use it.*

Koneka did not move. *It is a sword.*

Obviously. An iron sword, with a Bane of Arthropods enchantment. It is a very excellent weapon. Two of your noble young comrades donated it to the cause. You may thank them after the great battles to come.

But it cannot be a sword, Cruxunit Kraj.

Commander Kraj! Speak correctly to your elder! thought Captain Tamat loudly. But Kraj himself remained calm. The young creature seemed to amuse him with her careful thoughts.

Oh? And why not?

Because you want me to use it. I cannot use a sword.

Of course you can. Whoever told you such nonsense?

One of the other enderfrags piped up, *Taskmaster Owari says that the enderman must not stoop to weapons as the human does.*

Yet another fragment dutifully recited last week's lesson: *Weapons are the tools of Order. They must be crafted according to precise and Orderly instructions. Humans use them to shape and control the world.*

Koneka finished the recital. *The enderman is superior. The Great Chaos needs only the power of our fists, which can never be lost, or shattered, or smelted into something else, or stolen from you.*

Commander Kraj glanced over the crowd of young ones. His eyes met those of Taskmaster Owari. The Taskmaster quite clearly did not approve.

I see, Kraj thought finally. *May I present a counter-argument?*

Taskmaster Owari gave her permission.

Who is your sparring partner, Fragment Koneka?

Koneka pointed to a young enderfrag called Nif in the front row.

Hit him.

Koneka hesitated again. She glanced up at Owari.

Do not look at Owari! Look at me! I am your commander. The Mouth of the Great Chaos has given me dominion over all the forces of the endermen and charged me to create the greatest army the End has ever known or will ever know. What has Owari done? Taught juveniles not to break their toes when they kick one another.

I thought you said that the fragments would not be required to fight, Commander Kraj, Owari thought icily.

I have changed my mind. I will leave no tool unused in the great struggle. Look at me, Fragment Koneka. It is Left-Hand Human-Punching day is it not? So pretend he is a human. Hit him. Show me your left-hand punch.

Koneka dashed forward and struck Nif in the arm. Kraj was right, they did this all the time. Sparring was everyone's favorite. Nif flushed red, but the damage was minor. Koneka didn't hit hard unless it was Unlimited Brawling day. Nif rubbed his arm. He smiled at Koneka, so she would know he wasn't mad that she'd punched him in front of the whole Dome. Nif wouldn't ever be mad at Koneka. They'd been friends since they'd first been replicated. They chased endermites together across the islands and pelted each other with chorus fruits and made fun of Taskmaster Owari behind her back. When it was just the two of them, they were just smart enough for uncomplicated fun like that.

Kraj laid his hand gently on Koneka's shoulder. *Now, take the sword.*

Koneka didn't want to. Everyone knew she didn't. Her thoughts shone clear and bright. The sword was unnatural. The sword was Order. The sword was *human*.

And the sword would probably kill Nif.

Koneka picked it up suddenly. Decisively. She didn't know why, really. She just did it. It felt heavy and cold and foreign in her hand. Her thoughts felt heavy and cold and foreign, too. Kraj was beaming at her. Taskmaster Owari seemed disconcerted. Nif was sweating spores. Koneka's arm was moving into an offensive position already, all on its own.

We are just sparring though, right? Nif thought shakily. *Koneka? It is just practice.*

Hit him, Kraj commanded.

It will hurt him.

We are at war, Enderfrag Koneka. The human threat will not stand here asking questions. Humans will act. They will fight. They will stab. Everyone is going to hurt, sooner or later.

Koneka looked back and forth between Nif and Kraj helplessly. Then her mind filled with the desire to cut Nif down. She didn't know where the idea came from. It just suddenly arrived in her brain, in full color. She raised the iron sword high in the air.

This is unnecessary, Commander Kraj! The angry, brittle thoughts of Taskmaster Owari sliced through the image in Koneka's mind. It dissolved as though she had never thought such a thing. She shook her head as though it were buzzy with bees.

Kraj's mindscape became a wordless snarl.

Surely we need every enderman for the fight ahead, thought Owari soothingly. *Just as you said.* She chose her ideas slowly and carefully. *We cannot afford to waste young, strong warriors on such a simple demonstration.*

The snarl vanished as quickly as it arose. Commander Kraj

laughed loudly into the minds of the Enderdome. *Of course, Taskmaster! You did not think I would allow my enderfrags to actually delete each other? How foolish of you. We forgive you, naturally, you could not know the powerful mind of a cruxunit and a commander. You must take things as they seem, rather than as they are. My demonstration is already complete! Enderfrag Koneka showed no reluctance at all in punching her sparring partner. But she froze when asked to use a weapon on him! Because she knows the weapon is better in every way than a fist. She knows her blows will leave the enemy standing, but a sword will destroy him. Why then, fragments, would we shun weapons when faced with the human horde? Why would we volunteer to be weaker and slower and more defenseless? Ridiculous! Now, we have a number of items to choose from here. Everyone select something and we will begin the real Enderdome. I award you all the rank of private—except you, Koneka. You have already done well. You will be my lieutenant.*

A scuttling sound echoed behind Kraj. In one fluid movement, he snatched the sword out of Koneka's hand, spun, and flung it hard toward an endermite crawling across the courtyard. It died the instant the blade touched its skin.

Bane of Arthropods, Kraj thought with tremendous satisfaction. *How marvelous.*

The other enderfrags ran across the courtyard to Kraj's officers and began to sort through the inventory of Fin and Mo's lovingly collected weapons and armor. Koneka just stared at her sword wobbling a little where it stuck in the stone as the endermite went up in smoke around it.

Why did I imagine killing Nif? she thought. *Why would I ever imagine that?*

But no one was paying attention to her anymore. The commander and the Taskmaster faced each other in the sparring courtyard.

I do not approve of this, Commander.

I do not care what you approve of. I am commander. I speak for all of us.

That is not our way. When enough of us are gathered, we speak together. There is no need for a commander.

But there is. There is, Taskmaster Owari! There has always been, it is just that none of us was clever enough to see it. When we gathered on the dragon's island, so many minds all unified at last, I finally knew the truth. The path we should have taken all along. We have always suffered at the hands of the human world. But why? Why should we suffer at all? Why should they rule the Overworld, where such riches lie, while we skulk and guard our few camps here in the End, where so little grows? If they can take our lands, our resources, we can take theirs, too. We have not, because we hold ourselves back with silly rules like not using weapons or following commanders. I will make us better. You must see that. Under my reign, we will fly, Owari. We will fly to the Overworld and stop every bad thing from happening. I will defeat even the rain.

The Taskmaster's eyes flashed dangerously. *What you are talking about is blasphemy, Kraj.*

I disagree.

Reality does not care whether you agree with it. You have elevated yourself. You have created an army, with ranks and duties. You intend to emulate humans. There is no Chaos in this. No divine fire of unpredictability. You have become a servant of Order.

Silence your foul mind or I will silence it for you, Kraj hissed.

Taskmaster Owari folded her long hands behind her back. *You have done more than that, I suspect. Little Koneka was seconds*

away from killing Nif. She would never do that in the Enderdome.
They are practically a paired unit already. There are never fewer
than fifty fragments stacked here at any time. Our minds are always
calm and civilized in the Dome, so that they can learn. Yet she
would have done it. Murdered her friend. And look at your officers!
They should be as clever as you, traveling all together. A gang of
Krajs! But they obey you no matter what you say, meekly, without
argument. Why should they? They are not your End, your family.

Kraj smiled in his mind. A huge and ghostly smile. *I am a*
cruxunit. In the Beginning of the End I divided myself voluntarily,
to create a family. Perhaps they simply respect their elder.

I am a cruxunit, too, Kraj. We are equals. Or have you forgotten
everything about the Beginning of the End? You must have, to call
it the Beginning. The End existed before us and will exist long after.
Will you next claim to have built these cities? Your pride is ugly,
Commander. *I have taught generations of enderfrags and none of*
them obeys me meekly because I am an ancient cruxunit. What
have you done, Kraj? What have the Forces of Order promised you?

Do not be angry with me, Taskmaster. We are on the same side.
We both want only to survive. The humans are coming. Let us have
no conflict amongst ourselves. Kraj reached out a slender, dark
hand and gripped Owari's shoulder in a gesture of friendship.

The commander's hand was wet and cold. It tingled, then it
began to burn.

That end ship tethered out in the darkness was really something
extraordinary, Taskmaster, Kraj mused. *I could never have imag-*
ined those twins capable of such . . . industry. I think perhaps it was
a mistake to keep them out of the Dome. They will serve us well in
the fight. Better still if you had trained them. But how could you
have known? How could I have known?

Commander Kraj pulled his hand away. His fingers were covered in a scrap of leather, to protect his skin. A scrap of leather stained dark cobalt blue. Owari swayed unsteadily.

Yes, truly extraordinary, Kraj thought. *I found this among the other potions. So many potions. This one is a Potion of Weakness. It slows you down, makes you stupid, makes you miss your attacks. And, if a strong, powerful mind is nearby? Well. A weak mind is easy to control. Suggestible. What a wonderfully useful thing. You may call it blasphemy, but you cannot say Order is not effective. Like the sword and the fist. The fist is holier. But I choose the sword. There will be plenty of time to let Chaos reign when I own the human world from top to bottom. It is only logical. How else can we be safe, unless they are gone? If a little Order can get the endermen where we should be, why not embrace it, for a little while?*

Owari stared woozily into Kraj's sharp purple eyes.

Yes, the Taskmaster thought, as though it had been her own idea all along. *Why not?*

The ancient cruxunit walked slowly across the courtyard to join the other officers.

CHAPTER FIFTEEN

A LITTLE RAIN

Mo.

The thought wafted in through the window of Jax's grand house like steam off a warm cake. Familiar and comforting and sweet.

Mo.

Mo was asleep. In a *bed*. A bed that didn't *explode*. She'd always slept curled up on the floor of the ship with her brother like stray cats. But Jax insisted she sleep in a proper bed. It was safer, he promised. In the morning, they'd try a few witch's potions on her and see if anything sparked her memory. She didn't really like the sound of "witch's potions." Who was this witch? Did she run a clean kitchen? Could Mo trust her potions? Could Mo trust Jax? What was a witch, anyway? But Jax was determined to know where she'd gotten the egg and the totem. Mo certainly wanted to know, too. Maybe. Maybe she didn't. If she'd done something terrible to get them . . . maybe it was better not to know. He hadn't taken them away from her. She appreciated that, at least. Jax was very strict about that sort of thing, clearly. Her loot was her loot, and he wouldn't take it. If Jax was everything else Kraj and the Mouth had ever said of humans, he still had some morals. More than Kraj did.

On the end of the bed, right next to her feet, Loathsome the zombie horse snored phlegmily. Her big moldy nostrils flared with every gurgling breath.

Muuuumma, Loathsome snored contentedly. *Braaaains.*

Mo.

Mo was dreaming. The thought tried to find her in the dream. Mo was dreaming of the ender dragon's island. Only it wasn't the ender dragon's island. Not quite. The same yellow sandy rock. The same obsidian pillars. The same crystal flames in silver cages. The same tall, black endermen floating in their mist of hazy purple telepathic particles. The same gorgeously horrible, horribly gorgeous massive lizard soaring through the sky. Only the sky wasn't black. It was bright blue, like the sky in the Overworld. The sun shone down like a lamp. Mo stood on top of one of the pillars. An enderman was standing next to her. But it wasn't Fin. Or Kan. Or Karshen. Or Lopp.

It was Kraj.

Without saying a word, Kraj reached out and grabbed her arm. It came off in his strong hand.

Poor Endless trashfrags, Kraj thought. He put his hand on her other arm. It came off as easily and painlessly as pulling up a blade of grass. *You will find that in periods of war, niceties are a waste of time.* He reached down and pulled off her leg at the knee.

And almost everything is niceties, in the end. Still there was no pain. But Mo stumbled, trying to keep her balance. She tried to tell him not to take her leg. She needed it. The army didn't need *both* legs, did it? But no words came out of her mouth. Commander Kraj stretched out his fingers to take the other leg. *Everyone must give something up so that the End can go on.* Mo hopped away. Kraj floated toward her. He was so tall.

Mo dreamed she heard voices coming from far below. Different people, all talking at once.

Go, go, go! Go without me! I'll be fine!

Greenboy. My greenboy.

I can feel it coming. Like a tsunami. First the water retreats, and for a minute you think everything is going to be okay. Then it rises up and washes everything away. I love you.

I love you.

Then, suddenly, the enderman towering over her wasn't Kraj anymore. He had strange blue eyes in his giant ender head. Blue eyes and a necklace of ender pearls. Mo knew those eyes. It was Jax, trapped in an enderman's body. Just the same way Mo had been trapped. Ender-Jax handed her arms back, then her leg. You did it, he whispered to her. *You killed him. I'm so proud of you.*

Mo.

Mo woke up with a little scream. "I didn't do anything," she moaned.

Loathsome looked up at her out of one droopy, goopy eye. The demon pony went tense, ready to protect her mother from anything.

But there was nothing there. Just the quiet little thought in her head.

Mo.

The human girl looked all around the dark bedroom. Not even a torch to see by. She stood up on the narrow wooden bed on her tiptoes and peered out of the window. Mo stared down and out into the moonlit valley where Jax lived. Soft green grass. Hard grey hills. Lilacs and poppies waved back and forth in the night breeze. They shone black and grey in the shadows instead of violet and red.

Mo, it is me.

Two bright green eyes opened up in the dark. Kan was down there in the grass, two stories below, looking up at her. He was sitting on his note block.

Hi, Kan thought.

Hi, thought Mo.

Brains, thought Loathsome decisively.

"Shhh!" Mo hissed.

Brains, the pony whispered.

Kan, what are you doing here? If Jax catches you, he'll kill you. Actually kill you.

I will catch him first.

He killed Lopp.

Kan blinked. *Really? She is . . . just dead?*

Mo nodded. *He took her pearl.*

What a perfect . . . human, Kan spat.

No, you don't understand. She was going to kill me. She was all by herself. Her mind was nothing but murder and I tried to talk to her but she was just . . . dangry. Like Fin always says. You know what we're like alone.

Oh? What are we like?

Mo went pale. She couldn't be included in "we" anymore. She wasn't "we." She wasn't "us." She was just a human like all the other humans, and Kan was supposed to be her enemy.

Kan relaxed. *Never mind,* he thought. *Sorry. Do not listen to me. It does not matter.*

Mo looked out beyond the shadowy patch where Kan stood. *Wait.* You're *all by yourself,* she thought hesitantly, not wanting to offend him. *Are you . . . ok? Are you Kan?*

I know, it is weird. Turns out I have been by myself a while now. But I am just me. He held up his long black hands in the dark. He was completely calm. His thoughts felt as cool and collected as a glass of water. *See? No raaar. Just Kan.*

What do you mean "for a while now"?

Mo. You are not an enderman. Neither is Fin. Grumpo sure as dark and the Great Chaos is not. So if you think about it, I have been all by myself every time the three of us have been together. And I have played my note block better than anyone alive and not killed anyone or eaten my own toes or walked off an island into nothing.

Mo felt a chill in her guts. She was human. That explained a lot. So what was Kan? What could explain this? *Huh. That's . . . uh . . . that's something we should talk about, don't you think?*

Probably. But there are more important things going on right now. At the moment, I am choosing to believe I have enderman superpowers and leave it at that. I came to rescue you. Kan winced. That sounded stupid. It felt stupid. But he had. He'd come all the way up to the badlands for her.

Rescue me? But I'm fine. We're fine. Jax is gonna experiment on me tomorrow.

Kan blinked again. *Sounds great. Torture after lunch, then? Maybe a little slice and dice before bedtime? Mo, even for a human, Jax is bad news.*

He says it's to get my memory back. He's said a lot of things, Kan. I don't know what to believe. He's pretty mad at me right now, to tell you the truth.

Well, believe that I am your friend. That I have always been your friend. I will always be your friend. I have always told you the truth. I have never experimented on you. And I will never leave you behind. Also believe that it is probably a bad idea to let someone who is pretty mad at you experiment on you. Mo blinked. That had never occurred to her. That Jax might hurt her on purpose. No one in the history of Mo's life had ever meant her harm. The worst thing they'd ever done was simply to leave her alone with nothing. *Let us go. I know where a portal is. If you are quiet, we can just slip back through before he knows what happened. We will be careful so he cannot follow us back to the End. He will not be able to kill ED. Or anyone else. And it will not matter what he is mad at.*

But the others . . .

I do not think they are quite the same. They have all just been hanging out with Fin on this weird little island by the ship. They are not hurting anybody. None of them killed Lopp. They have not killed anyone. It is strange, honestly. I keep expecting them to start killing and they continue to kill nothing. I do not know what to make of it.

Are you spying on them?

An image opened up in Mo's mind. A beautiful banner unfurling on one of the tallest violet towers of Telos. Kan's smile.

I am a spy after all, he thought, proud of himself. *Grumpo let me hide in his box.*

Mo practically jumped over the windowsill in excitement. WHAT? *Grumpo NEVER lets anyone in that box! He hates Fin least of anyone and all he's ever let him do is stand a foot away and put one finger on the lid. And he still bit him.*

You two ran off without a word to Grumpo and I think he is feeling very frightened. If a shulker can feel frightened. Where did you find Grumpo anyway? *I have never met a shulker like that. You know they do not usually talk, right? They do not usually anything. I guess I never thought about it till now. Till everything.*

I never met an enderman like you either. And I bet until about a day and a half ago, you'd never met a human like me. What was it like in that box?

Crowded. Dark. A weird odor. He refused to let me light a torch. And he said something strange. He said, Stay in here with Grumpo forever. We can hate everything together. *Is that not the oddest idea? I left the box quickly after that.* Mo, Kan thought, sliding his eyes off toward the other windows. Jax's window. *I do not want to keep talking like this. Come out. Come with me. Come home. It is okay. I am not mad. It is not your fault. I understand that now. I was just upset. I just . . . I wanted my life to make sense. And it still does not. But it is not about me right now. We need to make your life make sense. And you can only do that with us. Your twin and your ship and your shulker and me. Your End. Jax is not your End. He is just a hunter who wants to catch something unique. All hunters do. And you are very unique.*

Mo looked over her shoulder toward the bedroom door. *I don't know,* she thought. *Maybe he has answers. You don't know what's happened. I had something in my pocket. I didn't even know about it. A couple of things.* The totem she didn't really understand. It didn't matter to her at all. The pearl she understood completely. But she couldn't tell Kan about it. There were some things too wrong to forgive. And what if he saw Lopp's pearl and knew who it came from? He'd never speak to her again. *One of them is a dragon's egg and Jax said there's only one way I could have gotten one . . . and if I got it that way I should never, ever go back to the End no matter what forever.*

I do not care what you have in your pockets. There is nothing you could have done that would change my mind about you. Mo, you turned out to be a human being *and I am still your friend. I am still here for you, in the awful old Overworld where I do not want to be at all.* Kan held up his long, black arms to her. *I do not want you to be experimented on. Come home. Remembering is so over-rated.*

Mo looked over at Loathsome. She patted the horse's greasy hair. She could see Loathsome's huge heart not beating between two gleaming ribs.

Mumma, saaaaaame, the zombie beast thought.

You're right, love. We are the same. *Kan and me and Fin. And you. And Grumpo. And the ship. And home. I don't know how you can be so smart. You were only just born. Or died. However it works. Either way. Both ways.*

Loathsome winked one milky, dead eye. *Brains,* she thought.

I'll climb down, Mo thought.

Kan shook his dark head. He held out his slender fingers toward the stone wall.

A block disappeared.

He lifted his fingers a little higher.

Another block vanished.

All hail the Great Chaos, Mo thought. And in Kan's mind, the image of a golden chestplate glinting in the evening light of the End bloomed. It was Mo's smile.

She held out her hand toward the windowsill. Human or not, the little violet particles still danced around her fingers, more faded and paler than they used to be, but still there.

The stone shimmered and hissed away into the air. Mo stretched out her arm again and erased another square of wall.

May the Great Chaos smile upon you, thought Kan, as the castle disappeared around him.

Block by block, the enderman and the human moved toward each other, making a staircase out of the remains of the wall as they went. Mo stepped down. Kan stepped up. The torches over the moat glowed golden. Jax's house opened up all around them. And when you lay open to the world, strange things could happen that would never find you if you stayed locked up behind orderly walls. Strange things like an enderman rescuing a girl and her zombie. This was the whole purpose of the Great Chaos. That was how Mo knew it was the right thing to do. Human or not, she still believed.

In her infinite pocket, the dragon egg glowed coldly.

Kan grabbed Mo's hand.

I didn't need rescuing, you know, she thought. *I could have just left anytime.*

Kan shrugged awkwardly. *Okay. It is the thought that counts? Can we at least tell Fin I rescued you, though? Very bravely?*

Mo laughed in the quiet between their minds. *Sure, Kan.*

Come on, he thought. *I feel pulled toward the nearest portal. I think I can sense the eyes of ender . . . but we have to be fast. It will be daylight soon. We will teleport. That is easiest. Ready?*

Mo pulled back, frozen. Kan still thought of her as she had always been. It hadn't occurred to him yet that humans couldn't teleport. That she must not've been doing it on her own. And Mo couldn't tell him. She just couldn't. He wouldn't understand. He'd just know that the ender pearl she'd used to teleport all over the End, all during their childhood, used to be somebody's heart, and he'd hate her for it. She wouldn't even let herself think about it. Kan would see the shriveled, dying ender pearl in her mind.

What is wrong?

Nothing. Um . . . Loathsome can't teleport. So. That. Is what's wrong.

Oh, right.

Loathsome burbled. A spit bubble swelled up on her lips and popped. But she didn't neigh. Zombies know how to be quiet. Occasionally.

Mumma, the pony wheezed. *Reeeeeins.*

Kan winced. There were sores and moldy streaks all along the horse's back. But she'd be faster than they could manage on foot by a long shot.

Mo hopped up onto Loathsome's back. It wasn't the nicest. It was a little wet and a little cold and a little slimy. But Loathsome was a little hers, so Mo didn't judge her. She pulled Kan up behind her.

I came to rescue you, he thought huffily. *I should ride in front.*

My horse, my seat preference, Mo thought. *Exits to the side and rear of the minecart.*

What? Kan thought, confused.

I . . . I don't know. What a strange thing to think. I don't know where it came from. What's a minecart?

How should I know? You thought it.

Mo shuddered in the dark. The moon came out from behind a cloud. It lit up Loathsome's green and undead mane. The horse took off away from Jax's great house into the hills, leaving nothing but hoofprints behind her. Neither Mo nor Kan looked back.

They rode for half an hour before Kan squeezed his knees against Loathsome's flanks. The zombie stopped obediently, though she narrowed her eyes and growled a little. Kan wasn't her mumma, and he shouldn't tell her what to do. Endermen had brains enough to eat.

It is here, he thought. *In that spot, but far under the ground. I can sense the portal.*

Kan pointed a short ways off, toward an area with a sand dune on one side and an overhanging cliff on the other, surrounded by huge leafy trees. Mo couldn't see any cave or passage underground, but she trusted Kan. If he said it was there, it was there.

The moon dimmed and vanished. Thunder cracked in the distance. Somewhere behind them, Mo and Kan heard the little speckled sounds of rain starting to fall.

Oh no, Kan thought in terror. *No, no, no.*

The cliff! Mo thought quickly. *Get under it! It'll be enough, the grass hangs over the edge and there's a little hollow there, it's almost a cave. You'll be fine.*

Loathsome ran for the cliff. Endermen cannot bear water. For them, water is death. Kan's breath came in great, hitching gasps. He teleported instantly off the horse's reeking back and appeared in the sandy patch beneath the overhang. Loathsome galloped full tilt after him.

The first drops started to fall.

Mo dismounted. She stood there in the grass, outside the safety of the cliff. The rain fell in big, loose drops onto her warm human skin. It fell harder and harder. She was soaked. She was soaked and it didn't hurt at all. It felt amazing. The crackle of ozone in the air, the smell of fresh greenery in the wind, the excitement of the thunder. All the little tiny hairs on her arms stood on end. But it didn't *hurt*.

Of course it didn't hurt. Mo raised her hands up as far as they would go and looked up into the stormy sky. All that fear, all that grief, all that hatred of the rain that had killed her hubunits washed away. It had never happened. Whoever her parents were, dead or alive, it wasn't rain that had taken them from her. Rain was just water. Cool and wet and sweet. She laughed and spun around. Rain wasn't death. It was *wonderful*.

But then she stopped laughing.

Kan stared miserably at her from under the little cliff. Shivering, frightened, trapped. Rain trickled down off the overhang into a growing puddle. One toe in that puddle and Kan would fade away, leaving only a pearl behind, like a thousand other endermen. The human and the enderman stood helplessly, separated forever by who they were. They'd been able to fool themselves until right that second. That nothing had changed. That Mo could teleport and Kan could survive in the Overworld. That they were still the same people they'd always been. Still an End. But Mo and Kan were nothing alike. They could never be alike.

"We'll go as soon as it stops," Mo said awkwardly. "I'll carry you to the stronghold."

Kan said nothing. He watched the sky. After a long while, he took out his note block, set it on the muddy ground, and began to play. His music filled up the field and the night, sad and sweet and strange. The music of the End echoed through the Overworld for the first time.

Mumma, groaned Loathsome as water dribbled through the holes in her body into the mud. *Raaaaain.*

Yeah, baby, answered Mo as the delicious, delightful storm drenched her from head to foot. *Sure is something, isn't it?*

CHAPTER SIXTEEN

UNDER COVER OF NIGHT

"Let me get this straight," said Roary. The night void of the End yawned behind her. The beginnings of the city Jess planned to build stood out brightly against it. "You've got all those books in your ship, hundreds of them, by my count. And you've never read *any* of them."

Fin shrugged. "I told you, they're enchanted. All got some kind of high-level Unbreaking enchantment on them. I don't know how to get it off. Do you?"

"Grindstone," Roary answered instantly.

"Grindstone," Jess said at the same time.

"Grindstone," said Koal.

"Fine," snapped Fin. "You're all so much smarter than me. It's not like Mo and I didn't try, you know. We didn't have a manual. We did our best. It's not my fault, either. The endermen didn't teach us. How am I supposed to find out about stuff like that if I wasn't taught it?"

The humans shifted uncomfortably. None wanted to tell the poor kid that they'd never gone to school. Or had a manual. Maybe things were just harder in the Overworld, so you had to sort yourself out faster. The kid'd had a hard enough day. Night. Whichever.

"If you didn't know what was in them, why'd you keep so many?" Koal asked.

Fin clenched his jaw. He didn't like having to answer for how he spent his time. Not to strangers. It was *his* time. "I like collecting things. I like the feeling of having *enough*. More than enough. Enough for anything that could ever happen. I hope I die with a full inventory, because that would mean nothing was ever bad enough that I had to use it all up. It makes me feel safe. It doesn't matter what's in the books or that I can't disenchant them. Eventually, if I collect enough things, one of them'll be the thing that will fix the books so I can read them. The Great Chaos will provide."

"I wouldn't think the Great Chaos would be big on books," Jesster said wryly. Fin had explained about all that. Jess didn't like it. Chaos made her nervous. Plans were so much better. "Books are pretty much the Orderliest."

Fin opened his mouth to dig into the religious philosophy of his former people, but Roary cut in.

"Where did you even *find* so many? I don't think I've ever seen so many books in one place outside a real library. It must have taken years."

Fin looked out into the night and blinked slowly as he thought about it. It was *very* eerie to think about. His brain kept sliding off it. He tried to think about the books, but he just didn't want to think about the books, even though he *did* want to think about the books and remember where they came from. It gave him a headache. "You know, I don't really know where we found them. It's weird. I can remember the day I found my Frost Walker boots, my Loyalty trident, the chestplate I use to make popcorn. I can even remember the day Kan found his note block. But I can't remember ever finding a single book. Not one. Not once. And we have hundreds, so shouldn't I remember something about *one* of them? But I don't. They were just . . . always there. From the beginning. Before we found our first sword out there in the islands, the ship was already full of those books."

Roary's eyes lit up. "That sounds like a clue," she said eagerly.

"God, Roary, you're such a dork." Koal put his hands on his hips mockingly. "Sergeant Roary, Kid Detective! That sounds like a *clue!*"

"Shut up, Koal," Roary said affectionately. "End ships usually have shulkers and a couple of treasure chests. They do *not* usually have a mountain of unopenable books. That's not a thing! And how many books have you seen anywhere else in the End? This is not exactly Booktown. Endermen aren't what you'd call serious intellectuals. We have no idea who you are or how you got here, Fin, and that's the first thing you've said that sounds like it might be a—stop snickering, Koal—clue. A path to some answers, are you happy? Ugh, take things seriously for once."

"I could make you a magnifying glass and a stupid hat, if you want." Koal laughed.

Roary threw up her hands and gave up on him. "Fin, it's not just that it would be cool to find out how a human managed to become an enderman and forget how they did it in the first place.

I *need* to know. We need to know. Because if it happened to you, it could happen to us, and I'm not going to get stuck wandering around here for years calling shulkers my BFFs. Ew. This is an operational imperative. We have to disenchant those books and see what's in them. And if it's just cookie recipes, well . . . I don't know. We hope Jax and Mo come back with something. We'll cross that bridge when we come to it. Right now, this is our best bet."

"So . . . do you have a grindstone?" Jess asked Fin.

"Well, I *did*, but Commander Kraj and Corporal Murrum and Captain Tamat have it now. In Telos, with the rest of the armory. I assume."

Roary thought about it. "Telos is big. It's the biggest end city I've ever seen. We gave it a wide berth when we came through. Not worth it. But we have a local guide. I think two of us could get in and out pretty quickly."

"No way," said Fin. "You don't understand. You think you're sneaky. That you're just playing games down here. The End was waiting for you. We knew you were coming by the *taste of the air*, Roary. Yesterday every enderman here was assembled to fight you. And they're still fired up and ready for war. The only reason they're not here now is that no one has come to check on Mo and me, so no one knows you're here. But they'll come soon. Someone will. Looking for Kan or looking for us. Karshen or Kraj. Sooner or later they'll wonder where we went. At the very least, they'll want to tell us they're not going to give our stuff back."

"You don't know that," Jesster tried to reassure him.

"I don't *know* it. But it's still true," mumbled Fin.

Koal rolled his eyes in disbelief. "A war? Against *us*? But there're *four* of us."

"Yeah, but they don't know that. All they knew was a portal was opening. They kind of thought it was . . . all of you."

Jess frowned at Fin. "*All* the humans?"

"Yeah. An invasion. They're just . . . waiting for the other side to show up. I tried to tell you that before. Why, is that a problem? I thought you and Jax liked fighting and killing."

"Well, there's fighting and then there's four on ten thousand," Koal muttered.

Fin started to laugh. He didn't want to laugh. He didn't mean to laugh. But it was all just so funny to him all of a sudden. The last few days of stress and misery and fear poured out in a flood of giggles.

"You don't even"—he gasped between bouts of hysterical laughing—"you don't even know how worked up they all are about you. They're so terrified of the big bad human army. They stripped the End for supplies to fight the oogey boogey human menace and you're just . . . you're just *tourists*. You're on vacation! Building sandcastles and hunting the local wildlife and then you're just gonna scamper off back home and tell your friends what a grand adventure you had. Take souvenirs! Write postcards! See the Magnificent End and Its Many Attractions! Ride the Ender Dragon! Play Whack-a-Shulker! Wish you were here!" Fin had to sit down. He could barely breathe. "We thought you were the scariest thing in the world." But then he thought about Jax, and ED, and how quickly his little universe had disintegrated once the humans set foot there. Everything he'd ever known really *was* ruined. It was just that everything the other endermen had ever known was still just fine. He and Mo were the only casualties of the war with the humans.

So far.

"I don't know," he finished softly. "Maybe you are the scariest thing in the world."

"What's wrong with being a tourist?" Koal shouted angrily. "Didn't you ever want to see anything but this stupid place with its stupid trees and its stupid cities and all its incredible stupidness? You should try being a tourist. It's *interesting*. It's *fun*. It's not *boring*. Traveling makes you bigger and wiser and cleverer and when you lie down in bed at night you have something to dream about. It doesn't hurt anyone. You shouldn't drum up an army just because someone takes their holiday in your neighborhood!"

"Jax is going to kill the ender dragon! It'll hurt the ender dragon plenty! And ED is my friend." Fin stopped and scrunched up one side of his face. "Well, not my friend. But it's not actively my enemy and that's pretty much the same thing!"

Koal looked down at his feet. "Yeah, ok, that's fair," he admitted. "But Jax isn't here and your 'not actively an enemy' is fine. For now."

"We can get in and out of Telos without this Kraj knowing about it," Roary said, choosing to ignore Fin's and Koal's outbursts. "You're forgetting that we came prepared. We've got pumpkins. We can move around the End just as well as you did for all those years, and no one will know, any more than they knew about you. In fact, we can all do whatever we came here to do, without getting caught, and go home at the end with no one the wiser. The endermen can go back to doing whatever it is that endermen do. Win-win-win."

"Except ED. I'm not going to let Jax do it," Fin said in as serious a voice as he could manage, having only started talking with his mouth a few hours before.

"We *have* to—" Koal started. But he didn't get to finish.

"You'll have to take that up with him when he gets back," Jess evaded. "Not our gig."

"But Telos!" Roary said, her dark eyes lighting up with the thrill of the mystery. "Telos can be our gig. It's a real honest-to-god spy mission. We'll sneak in, liberate your stash, and sneak out again. Under cover of night! Not that we have a choice. And if your army friends see us, they'll think we're just prepping, like them, right?"

"I guess . . . probably."

"Once we have a grindstone we can disenchant your books really fast," Jess assured him. "It's no problem, I've done it tons of times."

Roary nodded. "Maybe there's something in there that will help you remember who you are. Maybe the spell that took your memory is hiding in one of them. Or the spell to cure it. You could know everything that ever happened to you in just a couple of hours. Isn't that exciting?"

Fin thought about Mo. Where was she? He hated not knowing where she was. If she was okay. What she was doing. If he was making the right decisions without her.

"I suppose," he said, but he didn't feel it. What he did feel was a big ball of dread right in the pit of his stomach.

"Hey, yeah, you never know, maybe you'll find out something even more devastating than being a secret human!" Koal threw in cheerfully.

Fin thought he might be sick. *Come home, Mo! Yell at these guys with me! It's always better yelling as a team than yelling solo. Where are you?*

"I'll go with you, Fin," Jesster said kindly. "I'm the biggest and I have the best weapons. If we all go together, they might get suspicious. Four strange endermen they don't know sneaking around. Roary and Koal can stay and work on the palace. We don't want to fall behind."

Fin nodded. He had to *do* something. All this standing around and talking made him itch. He used to spend all day climbing and cruising between islands, without a care in the world. Now he was stuck arguing with strangers about strange things, no Grumpo, no Mo, no Kan, no purple popcorn, no nothing but them. *Do I really want to know?* he asked himself. *Maybe I should just go up to the Overworld with Mo and start living life human-style. Don't ask questions. Don't pry. Don't look a gift human in the mouth.* But no. He couldn't do it. He couldn't let things go back to the way they were. If he and Mo were human beings, then they weren't Endless. They weren't outcasts. They had a family somewhere. They had people. They had a world where they did belong. And that was worth finding. It had to be.

I can't go back. I can only start over.

One way or another, he had to know who he was and what had happened to him. Even if it was something terrible. Especially if it was something terrible.

Fin straightened his shoulders. His blue eyes shone in the dark.

"Okay, Jess. Let's go."

CHAPTER SEVENTEEN

WELCOME TO MY ED TALK

Kan, Mo, and Loathsome tumbled through the portal. Grey stronghold-stone and underground torches turned upside down, then inside out. They landed stomach-first, sprawled across the outcropping of sandy stone on the underside of the ender dragon's island. Mo was still soaking wet. Kan inched away from her, just to be safe. They could hear the vibrating roars of the great black lizard far above. The earth shook every time it bellowed fire into the dark. Even if they couldn't see it, they could feel it.

Mo stared out into the black sky of the End. She felt the rock under her fingers. She'd been gone only—what? Eight or nine hours? Half a day? More? Less? She didn't know. You never needed to tell time in the End. She didn't know what a proper hour was supposed to feel like. But it didn't matter how much time it was, it felt like a hundred years plus eternity. Nothing looked the same. Not after she'd seen the sun. Nothing could ever look the same again. The End seemed so small now. It looked back at her like a stranger.

Kan grimaced as he pictured the portal they'd just used. The twelve dead, hard eyes of ender that were stuck on to each block of the frame gleamed greyish green. Mo felt ill just looking at them. Loathsome thought they were just beautiful. The prettiest jewels she'd ever seen. She rather wanted to eat one. Loathsome looked at Mo for permission. She was so hungry. She was always just so hungry. Mo nodded.

The zombie horse squealed in delight and snapped at the eyes as they stepped through the portal. She chomped as fast as she could, chomping while falling, popping them like bubbles, slurping, crunching, munching, relishing. The eyes crunched like candy between her sharp yellow teeth.

Without those eyes, Mo figured Jax wouldn't be able to come through that portal. He'd have to hunt down yet another stronghold before he could track them down. As the trio regrouped safely back in the End, that thought at least was comforting.

Mmmmmumma, Loathsome hummed with satisfaction as she slurped up a bloodshot mess of eyeball off her blistered lip like spaghetti. *Veeeeiiiins.*

Yummy, Mo said as she fought to keep from throwing up. She couldn't remember ever having a mother, but she felt it was generally important for parents not to shame their children for their tastes. The baby was eating, that was the important thing.

Kan shuddered. He patted the horse. Carefully. Gingerly. Those teeth meant business. Loathsome went stiff. No one but Mo had ever patted her in her whole sixteen hours of life. The undead pony froze mid-snack. But Kan's hand was cold and hard and heavy. To a zombie, that feels very nice indeed. People who were not Mo were obviously bad and wrong, the horse knew. But at least one of them was . . . acceptable. Barely.

He wasn't that bad, Mo thought.

Who?

Jax. I think really he's just a kid like us. He likes to hit things and take things and do what he likes without anyone bothering him.

He likes to kill things, Kan corrected her. *He wants to kill the ender dragon.*

I know that's bad. But he gave me back my chestplate. Kraj likes to kill things and he stole it from me. And Kraj hasn't been a kid since the dawn of time.

You like him.

No, I don't. Mo sighed. *Right now, I like anyone who helps me make sense of all this insanity. He's one of only four humans I know. Five, I guess, counting Fin. At least he hasn't hurt me yet. If anyone I used to know down here sees me, they will. You know they will.*

Mo's green eyes filled up with tears. She remembered Lopp's face, twisted up and furious and cruel. Lopp, who once asked her if she needed a hubunit. She didn't want to see anyone else look at her like that. Not ever. Mo needed a hubunit now. But she'd never say so.

Kan put his arms around his friend. The pearl where his heart should have been pulsed fast, the way any human boy's heart would have.

I have an idea, he thought.

Is it to give up and hide forever with me and my horse?

No. Mo, someone, somewhere knows the truth about us. About

*what happened to you and Fin. About why I am . . . the way that I
am. There is not anything in the universe that somebody does not
know. Now, let us lay it all out. What do we know? Not much, I
admit.*

Me and Fin are human beings.

Therefore, you came from the Overworld.

*Sure, that's logical enough. Endermen come from the End, rain
comes from the sky, humans come from the Overworld. Ah! Therefore, we had to come down to the End at some point. With the
pumpkins on. Through a portal. Jax says that's the only way for a
human to travel between the Overworld and the End.*

*Right. And it had to be some time ago, because you and Fin and
I have all these memories of growing up together. And your pumpkins were not exactly fresh.*

Mo picked at her fingernails. How strange it was to have fingernails in the first place. *We also know that you aren't like other
endermen,* she thought. *You have green eyes. You can play music.
And when you're by yourself, you don't go halfwit berserker dangry
on everything. But you aren't wearing a pumpkin and you're not
human.*

Kan sighed. *I think your mystery is easier. I wish it were not.
Believe me. I never thought that more than anything in the world,
someday I would wish I were a human being with a pumpkin on his
head. But here we are. At least we have somewhere to start with
yours. I am just . . . a freak. A greenboy.*

Kan, don't say that.

It is true.

Mo touched his cheek. His skin felt like wet ink, even though
it was dry. *If you're a greenboy, I'm a greengirl,* she thought. *Our
eyes are exactly the same. If you're a freak, I'm a freak. Freak Club.
Population two.*

They were almost close enough to kiss.

You mean three, Kan thought bashfully. *Fin, too.*

Yeah, thought Mo, a little embarrassed. For the first time, she saw an advantage in *not* having telepathy. *Three. Sure. Fin, too.*

Kan's pearl thundered in his chest. Why had he brought Fin into it? What a fool he was. The moment had passed. The thing about telepathy was that you couldn't hide your feelings from anyone. Especially not from the girl you'd known all your life. He tried to hide how much her words meant to him. But she knew anyway. With telepathy, you couldn't put on a tough face. You could only change the subject. So he did.

So if you came to the End at some point, someone must have seen it. Everyone knew when Jax's portal was about to open. They knew right away. So if you came through a portal, somebody knew then, too.

Mo caught on to where Kan was headed with this. *So who's old enough to remember two humans coming through a portal years ago? Kraj, obviously.*

For once, I doubt he will want to regale us with tales of the past. Right now, he is not even Kraj anymore. He is Commander Kraj. The "commander" makes all the difference. One look at you and he will command you out of existence. And me for helping you. An earsplitting shriek broke through the air far above them.

Mo's thoughts lit up. *ED? The ender dragon?*

There is nothing in the End older than ED.

There is nothing in the End meaner than ED. It's not going to tell us what color my shoes are. Huh. I have shoes. I'm wearing shoes. Did you see my shoes?

I saw your shoes, Kan thought. *They are awful. I thought you said ED showed you where to find Loathsome's egg?*

Yeah, because the meanest people are the ones who are occa-

sionally nice. You can never totally hate them, since they really were so kind to you that one time a million years ago. So they can keep on hurting you while you wait for that one nice day to come around again. Also, it probably hoped she would eat me.

Brains, agreed Loathsome. Kan narrowed his eyes.

Let us go talk to it. Maybe today is a nice day.

Kan got up to start the climb up the rockface and over the lip of the island to the grand plain where the ender dragon lived.

Wait, Kan! Mo grabbed at him. *I can't.* The enderman hopped back down. *You know I can't.*

Why can you not?

Mo laughed. She pointed at her face. He still didn't get it. *No pumpkin. I look as human as I am. Have you ever seen the island not crawling with endermen? They'll see me. They'll kill me. And they won't even know it was poor little orphan Mo they killed.*

Okay, so we just teleport up to the top of one of the pillars. Easy. No one will see us up there.

Mo went pale. *I . . . I can't do that either.*

What? Sure you can. I have seen you teleport tons of times.

Mo slumped miserably. She couldn't look him in the eye. But she didn't need to. As soon as she thought about it, he knew.

Oh, he thought. *Oh. Um. Huh.* Kan looked away. Kan looking away was the most awful thing that had ever happened to Mo. And Mo was still in the middle of the worst day of her life. *Silly, I guess. I should have thought of that. It is . . . a lot to get used to. And everything.*

But Mo knew that under all that he was just wondering who it was. Whose heart and brain and soul she'd used as a public bus for so long. She hated herself. But should she hate herself? She didn't remember ever killing an enderman, let alone collecting their pearl. So the Mo that did that wasn't this Mo, right here, right now. That was another girl, a girl she'd never even met.

I suppose you are right, Kan answered her thoughts instantly. *This Mo is my friend. This Mo gave me a new note block when my hubunit destroyed mine. This Mo let me in and fed me whenever I ran away from home. This Mo loves a dead horse like her own baby. She could never hurt her people. Whatever that Mo did, I do not know her. All hail the Great Chaos, right? This whole mess is truly Its work. I have served the Great Chaos all my life. Why stop now?* Kan looked up, toward the ender dragon's lair. *Maybe the Great Chaos is just another way of saying life is crazy so you might as well get crazy, too.*

Kan sent his mind toward Loathsome's. He saw the infinite graveyard and the wiry trees and the sickly moon. He saw the gravestones of Loathsome's first memories, and now there were new ones. One said: YUMMY EYEBALLS. One said: DOUBLE MELON. One said: MUMMA'S FRIEND.

Stay here and we will come back for you, Kan thought to the graveyard. *Do not go anywhere till we get back. Do not even move.*

Remaaaain, Loathsome moaned.

Good, Kan thought. *Okay, Mo. Hold on to me? I will do it for both of us.*

Mo hesitated for a second. Jax the human being had just grabbed her. He hadn't cared what she thought or what she wanted. Kan the enderman was asking. Even though part of him was disgusted with her right now. What did that mean? Did it matter? She took a deep breath and stepped into the enderman's arms.

And quicker than she could let that breath out, they were standing on top of a towering obsidian pillar. A crystal flame crackled beside them in a silver cage. And far off on the other side of the island, the ender dragon flapped its enormous black-and-purple wings in the night, soaring toward them.

The dragon turned toward the eastern bank of pillars. It meant to pass right by. Its endless circling wouldn't be interrupted by a couple of brats. Mo and Kan held their breath. The ender dragon glided past on their left side—and turned its head.

ED looked at Mo. Directly at her. At her green eyes. At her black hair. At her human face.

And the ender dragon laughed.

It sounded like rocks banging down a mountainside and landing in a lake of fire. It sounded like a hundred people screaming at once. It sounded like stars dying. The ender dragon's thoughts exploded roughly into their heads.

Is it that time again already?

What? Mo thought, reeling from the force of the great reptile's mind.

It brings me pleasure to see the face of this primate uncovered. I did not expect you so soon. ED's Jurassic laughter banged around their skulls again. *Well done, child of the sun. Very quick. And the other one? He is likewise . . . revealed?*

Fin? I left him back at the ship. He's fine. He's safe.

So you knew? Kan spluttered. *You knew they were human all along?*

The ender dragon chortled. It sounded like thunder broken across the knee of the world. Its massive eyes slid shut. *I am the infinite lightning night-lizard at the end of the universe. I am the master of time and death. The fire of creation is my youngest brother. In my stomach, galaxies churn in cosmic acid and are digested into meaninglessness.* ED opened one vast violet eye. *You can't fool me with a pumpkin, dummy.*

Then you must remember! You must remember when they arrived.

ED flapped lazily around their pillar. *I do.*

Kan's excitement made the purple particles floating around his body glow like fireflies. *You must know what happened to them. You know why they do not remember anything.*

ED rolled onto its back midair and thrashed its mighty tail. *I do.*

Tell us! Tell her! Kan cried out in the space between their minds.

The ender dragon flexed its claws. *Nah,* it thought.

Why not? Mo pleaded. *I need to know. Who am I? Who is Fin? What should we do? Just leave and never come back?*

I would seriously consider it, if I were you, the dragon mused.

But this is our home. Up there . . . the way Jax talks about it . . . it's hard and lonely and everything wants to kill you. You have to know so much. No one helps you or tells you the right thing to do. There's an Order to everything, but you have to figure out what it is while creatures try to eat you alive. You're just . . . on your own. By yourself. Without an End. Mo's cheeks burned. Her thoughts went very quiet. *If we just found another couple of pumpkins, everything could go back to the way it was.*

You have come to the infinite lightning night-lizard for advice, ED thought as it dipped down and up again in a graceful loop the loop.

Yes!

I have never been asked for advice before. It is . . . annoying. Will it make you go away?

Yes, Kan thought. *We promise it will.*

Very well. Heed my words, mortal children! Life is very difficult and complex above and below. In the End and in the Beginning.

You must make your own decisions, and not rely on the world to tell you what to do so that you do not have to think. Nevertheless, there is a path, and you are always on it. Your choices created it. Your actions move it beneath your feet. You have crafted it as surely as any iron sword. The future is uncertain—up to a point. Then it is very certain. And inescapable. You are nearing that point now. And ultimately, the easiest, most correct, and wisest choice is to let me eat you.

Mo threw up her hands. *Oh, fine, if that's all the help you're going to be.*

ED shrugged its scaly shoulders. *You wanted my advice. I am selfish. As the universe is selfish. And hungry.* The ender dragon turned and flew straight at them. Then it stopped—and hovered. Not flying, simply existing without gravity. *I have known you a long time, Ultimo. It's really best if you let me eat you.* The dragon pouted. *You never let me eat you. You're no fun at all.*

Kan's mouth hung open in his sleek black face. *Ultimo? Who is Ultimo?*

But ED ignored him. *Do you know?* It asked Mo.

Know what?

ED sighed. *What a pity.*

You do not make any sense! Kan thought. Frustration burned in his green eyes.

The universe makes no sense, fragment. So I fit right in. Now get out. You promised. Leave me alone. I have much to prepare.

Wait, Mo thought. She trembled a little. ED was so big, so impossibly big. It could destroy her without even noticing. *I have to ask you something else. One last question.* She winced, then stuck her hand into her pocket and fished around. Jax had done it before, but she hadn't wanted to explore it herself. She had no idea what an empty block of space-time would feel like. She'd thought it would be creepy and unpleasant, and it was. Cold, dry, vast. It felt *grey*, if *grey* could be a feeling. Mo didn't like it. She felt her hand brush by many things she didn't recognize or understand by touch — and then her fingers fell on the thing she wanted.

Mo pulled the dragon's egg out of her pocket. She showed it to the ender dragon.

I have this, she thought nervously. *I have this and the human boy said . . . he said . . .*

Something hotter than the core of a planet ignited deep in ED's eyes. White ultraviolet flame popped in its pupils. Its breath quickened. The big, shiny black-and-purple egg was reflected in the dragon's eyes.

ED, Mo thought. She didn't know how it could be possible. But she had to ask. *Did I . . . did I kill you?*

With a scream of pure rage, the ender dragon reared back and vomited a thick, boiling stream of white-purple lavafire toward their pathetic little pillar.

Just before the flame reached them, Kan and Mo blinked out of existence.

The pillar erupted in a tornado of violet fire. It burned for a long time after they'd gone.

CHAPTER EIGHTEEN

TELOS

It was quiet in the city.

Fin felt like himself again. Tall, dark, and strong. Magenta eyes and a square jaw. Jess looked magnificent as an enderman. But all endermen looked magnificent. Fin had always thought they were clearly the most beautiful species, if you wanted to be objective about it.

"Just walk casual," Fin whispered. "And don't talk. You're supposed to be telepathic."

They stood on the edge of the city center. Black figures moved silently back and forth on the streets. Behind them, Fin and Jess could just see the shape of their ship floating off the island shore. He repeated the plan to himself. *In and out. In and out and back to the ship with the grindstone. Koal and Roary will meet us there. No problem.*

Jesster cocked her head to one side. "I'm not, though."

"Yeah, I got that," Fin said, distracted.

"That's very odd, don't you think?"

"No? You're human."

"So are you, Fin. But you communicate telepathically with Mo and Kan and I presume all the other endermen down here. I'm no different than you were when we met now. A human with a pumpkin on her head, which makes her look like an enderman. But I'm not an enderman. The pumpkin doesn't give me mind-reading powers. But you have them. Why? What's different?"

Fin rubbed his eyes, exasperated. "Knock me dead if I know, Jess. Yesterday I wanted to kill all humans. Today I am one. It's a lot. Let's just get this over with."

"Can you read my thoughts? Even if I can't read yours. Might be useful."

Fin tried. Nothing. He looked hard into Jess's mind. He searched for that image that always greeted a telepath when they tried to read a new person. Mo's ship, his open books, Kan's music, Koneka's family. In Jesster's head, he saw a perfectly-built cathedral. Beautiful, soaring, intricate, each stone in its place, the architecture precise and perfect. And the door was shut. She was human. She didn't know how to let her thoughts out or let others in. It was no use.

"No," he said.

"Too bad," answered Jess.

"Yeah."

"Where's the armory?"

Fin pointed to one of the fattest, tallest pagoda towers. Its purple roof forked up at the ends like the branches of chorus trees. All the buildings in the End looked alike, but not identical. Whoever built them liked things just so. The buildings matched the trees and the land. It all went together. Fin imagined that appealed to Jess the builder quite a bit.

"On the third level. Where the courtyard looks like a big mushroom. There's a door and a couple of shulkers there."

"Like your shulker?"

"No," Fin laughed. "Grumpo talks about biting me a lot. These actually will."

Jesster patted her hip. She wore a long diamond sword with a Fire Aspect enchantment on it. It was easily the most fantastic weapon Fin had ever seen. It would have looked so good hanging over Grumpo's box. Really tie the whole room together. Oh, well. He squeezed the handle of Koal's crossbow. The boy had lent it to him. Kraj had left them with so little to protect themselves.

"Hold on to me and I'll teleport us both right in," Fin said, holding out his hand. The ender pearl in his infinite human pocket was still good. He didn't know about it yet, because he hadn't had a moment to think about why he could teleport when he was just a human boy. But it lay there in his pocket anyway, putting out the last dregs of its energy for him to use.

Jess took his hand and the next thing either of them knew, they were standing inside the Telosian armory.

Fin and Mo's collection surrounded them. Fin gawped. The twins hadn't always kept their treasure organized and tidy, but at least they treated each item with care. Each thing was precious to them, even if it wasn't necessarily sorted into categories and stacked neatly. Nobody seemed to care about their stuff here. The room was huge, and everything Fin and Mo owned was thrown into great sloppy piles for anyone to take whatever they wanted without cleaning up after themselves. Weapons, armor, food, ore, potions. All just tossed together into a teetering, tottering trash heap. It glittered in the torchlight.

Fin had never really realized just how *much* they'd collected. The endersoldiers must have dumped it all back here when the war failed to get with the warring. Ready to be passed out again at a moment's notice. No *wonder* Kraj had commandeered it all. There was hardly anything in the enderman armory that *didn't* belong to them. If not for Mo and Fin, it seemed as though the End would have had to defend itself with a couple of small sticks and a stern expression.

Jesster opened her mouth to say something. Fin held his finger up to his lips. Funny how quickly and easily he made that gesture. Endermen never had to. No quiet like the quiet in the End. You didn't think with your mouth, so you wouldn't *shush* with it anyway. He'd never even seen anyone do it before. That he could remember, anyway, which wasn't saying much. Yet his finger flew up like he'd done it a thousand times. Instinct. *Habit.*

Jess pointed instead. She pointed to something dull and grey sticking out from under a small mountain of boots. The grindstone.

Fin glided across the room. He saw that Jess was impressed. His chest puffed out a little. Yeah, he could move like an enderman. Easy. Can't you? It wasn't really gliding. He just moved his feet in a certain quick way that looked like gliding. Instinct. Habit. Fin landed on the small mountain of boots. He reached down to wiggle the grindstone out of the trash heap as quietly as possible.

All hail the Great Chaos, Commander Kraj.

May the Great Chaos smile upon all your works and deeds, Corporal Murrum.

Fin's head snapped up toward the door. He glanced quickly at

Jess. She was standing out in the open in the middle of the armory, totally unprotected.

Hide! He thought. *They're coming! Kraj and Murrum are right outside!*

Jess blinked. She spread her hands. *What?*

Of course, she couldn't hear him. Ugh! Humans! Telepathy was just so much better than talking.

He tried to communicate with his eyes. Hard stare at Jess, hard stare at the door. Fin waved his hands as if pushing her back. Jess got the message. She ducked down behind a stack of water buckets and shovels just as the two grim, straight-backed soldiers walked into the armory. Fin was shocked to see one of them was Koneka, the juvenile enderman from the Enderdome. She looked . . . terrifyingly blank. Behind them more endermen followed. Kraj's personal brain squad was no longer just fifteen but fifty-nine soldiers. Kraj spoke only to Murrum. The rest were just there to make the commander cleverer. Living, breathing buffs.

You may deliver your report, Corporal Murrum. Kraj clasped his hands behind his back. He looked younger than he ever had. Power made him feel feisty, Fin supposed.

The portal is gone, sir.

Kraj looked benevolently at his underling out of the corner of his purple eye. But beneath that benevolence Fin felt the threat of the old enderman's anger.

Sire, Murrum. Not sir. It is sire, now.

Of course, sire, of course.

The Mouth of the Great Chaos blessed me with a royal title.

Corporal Murrum squinted and squirmed uncomfortably. *I thought you decided you should have a title. After you threw Eresha off a cliff because she ordered everyone to disband the army and go back to their homes on account of there being no human invasion after all.*

Commander Kraj's eyes bored into Murrum's. *Where did you hear this utter slander?* His thoughts thundered skull-to-skull.

S . . . s . . . some of the endersoldiers were talking after hours, that is all. Sire.

The Lord of All Endermen towered above the poor soldier. *You are MISTAKEN. Eresha is completely fine and resting comfortably at her house. It was she who chose to honor me. I am the humblest of all endermen. You know that, Murrum.*

I apologize deeply, my lord. The corporal shifted back and forth uncomfortably. *Well. In any event. The portal is gone, sire.*

Closed?

No, sire. Gone. Can you not feel it?

Of course I feel it! Do you think me a weak old enderman without his senses? Kraj exploded.

No, sire! Corporal Murrum cowered.

Fin's knees ached, crouching on the mound of boots. They were so slippery. He tried to hold on with his toes. If he moved, Kraj and his goons would hear.

The commander collected himself. *Humans are a clever, sneaky species. They specialize in deception the way spiders exercise the weaving of webs.*

Certainly, Commander, Murrum thought miserably. *Shall we start returning all this to the Endless fragments, then? Since the portal is gone and there is to be no war.*

Kraj looked at his manservant incredulously. *Return it? Whatever for? I need it. All of it. I cannot foresee a time when I will not need it. The human army would not just give up their ambitions, Murrum! No! The answer is simple. They are already here. Thou-*

sands of them. All around us, every moment. Why, they may be here in Telos already. In this very tower. In this very armory. We no longer feel the vibrations of the portal because they have shut it behind them. They do not intend to return home. No mercy, no surrender. What a cruel and heartless strategy from a cruel and heartless people.

The horror of the ruthless, calculating human heart settled down onto Corporal Murrum's shoulders. *How do you know, sire? Have you had word?*

*How do I know? Why, I have thought about it long and hard. I have imagined with the powers of my very good and fully stacked brain. And I have come to a logical conclusion. To me it is perfectly obvious that this is what has happened. I am the wisest enderman ever to live, after all. With my End—*Kraj gestured at the squad behind him—*no one can outthink me. No, Corporal Murrum, they are hiding their vast army among us. This cannot be denied.*

What will you do, sire?

Fin's legs screamed with the effort of holding still, keeping a grip on the grindstone, and not sliding down the pile of boots head over feet.

I will protect my people, of course. Do not fear. Pumpkins are just fruit, after all. And fruit can be . . . bruised. A dark smile showed itself between the words of Kraj's thoughts. *Everyone must be interrogated. One by one. I shall do this sad but necessary work. It is a sacrifice I am willing to make. We will uncover the saboteurs. We will punish them. But not as we usually do. That is too quick and merciful. We will make an example of them, so that every human ear in the Overworld hears what happens to invaders and plunderers in Kraj's Kingdom. And finally, the End will return to its great peace once more.*

And that's when it happened. Fin couldn't hold still any longer. If he just moved his right leg an inch or so, he'd be on flatter ground. He wouldn't have to hold on so tight. It'd be fine. He could do it without making noise. Sweet relief was just an inch that way. Fin slowly worked his foot over.

A pair of boots, held in place by his heel, slipped and started to slide down the pile. The boots had hard metal soles. Fin watched it happening with horror. He remembered finding that boot. On the outer islands, with Mo, a million years ago. They had a middling-strength Blast Protection enchantment on them. Pretty good boots, all in all. They were gonna make *such* a loud clang when they hit the ground. But he couldn't stop it. It was like it was happening to someone else. In slow motion. Fin was frozen.

Just then, a loud crash sounded from across the room. It totally swallowed up the sound of the old boot clattering onto the armory floor. Kraj, Murrum, and the fifty-eight soldiers behind them snapped to attention. The Lord of All Endermen shrieked like a teakettle devouring an air raid siren and shot across the room toward the water bucket skittering across the floor. The commander punched through the stack of water buckets with one black fist. Fin's heart jumped into his throat. Jess was back there!

But she wasn't.

Kraj kicked the other water buckets aside in a fit of rage.

Perhaps it was a stray endermite, sire. Murrum tried to calm his master.

Kraj shoved him aside. *You fool! THEY. ARE. HERE.*

How strange, Fin thought. Kraj was right. The humans *were* here. But he was so wrong, too. And Jess. She'd covered for him. Why? He wasn't anything to her. Why would she risk Kraj's wrath for him?

Fin suddenly saw a glint in the torchlight. Jess's eyes, between a teetering pyramid of gold and a barrel of cocoa beans. Not using telepathy was garbage, Fin decided firmly. How could humans stand it? If Jess had been like him, she could have just shown him what she wanted him to do in an instant.

Jess mouthed something. Fin squinted in the dim light, trying to make it out.

T-E-L-E-P-O-R-T. Go! Leave me.

No way! Fin mouthed back. *Not a chance!*

Ender-Jess, still slick and tall and black in the pumpkin helmet that disguised her so well, rolled her purple eyes. While Kraj raged at the water buckets, she crept out from behind the gold stash in complete silence. Jess slipped into formation with the fifty-nine-strong squad waiting patiently for their commander to come to his senses. Fin tensed when he saw Jess was standing right behind Koneka, but if the fragment noticed, she didn't give any sign. Fifty-nine was a lot of people. If you didn't count, you'd never know there was one extra. Fin sighed with relief. Jess was awfully good at this.

Sound the alarms, Murrum, Kraj roared. *Intruders! Endermen! With me! We will carve out the human menace!*

The brain squad came to attention. They turned as one to march out of the armory and into the city again, where they could rejoin the assembled forces of the End. *2-3-4-Hup!* In perfect time, they beat their path through the great door.

WAIT! The Lord of All Endermen's booming thoughts sliced through the minds of everyone in the room. Kraj seemed bigger and taller than ever as he flowed over to the troops. *Fee-fie-fo-fum,* he fumed, *I smell the blood of too many endermen!*

Kraj's dark hand fell upon Jess's shoulder.

I do not know you, soldier, he thought coldly. *What is your name? To what End do you belong?*

Jess stared up miserably into those boiling purple eyes. She couldn't understand him. She wasn't telepathic. To her, there was nothing in the armory but silence and danger.

I SAID GIVE ME YOUR NAME, SOLDIER! bellowed the thoughts of Kraj. *DO NOT DEFY YOUR LORD!*

But poor Jess could no more hear his words than she could hear Jax snoring in the Overworld. And if she spoke, no pumpkin in the world could hide what she was. She tried to inch her hand toward her sword.

Kraj's body flushed a deep, ugly red. His fury built and built until it was flashing and clanging inside him like a fire alarm. Fin couldn't believe it. With so many endermen around, Kraj should have been in total control of himself. The mindless rage of the berserker enderman should have stayed a million miles away. But there it was, plain as the red on the commander's face.

HOLD HER STILL! Kraj commanded. The ender squad obeyed without question. Koneka and another soldier seized her arms in a grip worse than any iron.

Sire! protested Murrum. *It is only a fragment!*

Are you really going to let her get caught right now? Fin asked himself. *Really, Fin? She tried to save you, and you're just going to watch him lose his mind on her? Move your feet, you coward.* But Fin couldn't. He wanted to. He really, really did. But his feet wouldn't do what he told them to.

Commander Kraj raised his fist into the air. In one terrible blow, he threw Jess across the whole of the armory. She crashed through a jumble of pickaxes and smashed into the far wall. Jesster sank to the ground. She moaned. She put her hand up to the back of her head.

It came away covered in shattered pumpkin.

Slowly, horribly, the helmet cracked and fell forward. Kraj and Murrum and fifty-eight endermen itching for war stared in fascination at their first human invader.

The scream of triumph that came out of Kraj in that moment could have shattered every glass bottle in the room, had he screamed out loud and not directly into all their minds until they ached. It sounded like the devil's nails down all the chalkboards in hell.

SEE? DO. YOU. SEE? I WAS RIGHT! AS RIGHT AS RAIN!

He went completely red and bent his head to charge Jess.

Fin's feet still wouldn't obey him. But that sound knocked the fear right out of him. Fine. If his legs wouldn't work, his arms would have to do. In one fluid motion, Fin pulled up his crossbow, yanked back the firing mechanism, and shot the Lord of All Endermen directly between the shoulder blades.

"All hail the Great Chaos," Fin whispered.

It happened so fast.

Kraj crumpled like an old umbrella. The red light of his anger went out. He hit the ground, but it hardly made a sound.

Oh no, Fin thought. *What have I done? Poor old Kraj. All his long, boring stories. I killed him. And his stories. I killed an enderman in the End. In his own land. What a good human I turned out to be.*

Two things happened at once. Corporal Murrum teleported in the direction of the crossbow bolt. And Jess leapt forward, flaming diamond sword in hand.

She mowed her way through the fifty-nine endermen bodyguards. Jess slashed left and right, slicing down and ripping up. It wasn't even a contest. Her blade cut through them like they were nothing.

No, thought Kraj weakly. *No, I need them!* Jess spun around and hacked another soldier in two. *Stop! I was right! Murrum! I was right! There she is! The human menace! Among us! I was right!* The endermen warriors tried to fight back, but they were no match. Some of them broke and ran. They blinked out, teleporting away, abandoning their commander. Koneka looked directly into Fin's eyes. One, two, three more went down.

By the Great Chaos, I believe I have journeyed too far and too swiftly, Koneka thought, just as she had that day they met out on the dunes above the Enderdome. But now her thoughts were the color of heartbreak and horror. She vanished in an instant, just as Jess's sword sliced through the space where she'd stood.

Kraj howled. *STOP! I need those soldiers! I need my End! I don't want to go back! I am the wisest of all endermen! I am . . . I am the wise . . .* The last of the squad sank to his knees and toppled forward. Jess panted in the middle of her carnage. The bodies were already disappearing, leaving their pearls behind.

Kraj's mind dissolved into a mindless scream of blind and thoughtless rage. And then it was silent too, and all that was left was a withered greenish-grey gem with a dull, dark shine deep within it.

Corporal Murrum bore down on Fin. He was alone now. *Nobody here but us humans*, Fin thought in a panic. Murrum's mind was a blank. All it wanted to do was kill. There was no one home behind those familiar purple eyes anymore. Murrum didn't see Fin, he didn't see anything. He just saw a target.

I had to, Fin thought, *I had to do it.* He closed his eyes, clutched the grindstone to his chest, and waited for the worst.

It didn't come. Endermen flooded into the armory in a black wave. They followed the death cry of Kraj into the room. As soon as the mass of them drew near, the stack initiated, and intelligence returned to the corporal's eyes. Intelligence, and cold hate.

Seize them immediately, Murrum ordered. Jess lifted her sword again but they rushed her too fast. She got one, two, and then they had her. *Keep the human for questioning. The fragment known as Fin murdered our beloved commander. We will also ask him a question. That question will be: What method of execution would you prefer?*

"Fin, just teleport away, don't risk yourself!" Jess yelled. What was the point of staying quiet now?

"I'm not leaving you!" he yelled back without thinking.

"Well, that's completely stupid!" Jess hollered.

Murrum staggered back, away from the sound of Fin's human voice. *Oh,* Fin thought. *Oh, I actually am an idiot. Endermen don't talk.*

Faster than Fin could regret his recent life choices, Corporal Murrum grabbed his head and slammed it into the wall. He felt the pumpkin crack and fall off. Fin turned a human face back to Murrum.

Fin? Murrum thought in total confusion. *It is not possible. I have known you since you were a young fragment. It is not true. It cannot be. Kraj . . . Kraj knew. He always knew. He was truly the wisest of us!*

I'm sorry, Murrum. And Fin was sorry. He really was. *Do I still get to pick how I'm executed?*

No, the corporal thought. The enderman turned to the crowd behind him. *Take them both to the Cage!*

Something big and hard and a lot like a fist hit Fin in the back of the head.

Lights out.

CHAPTER NINETEEN

REMEMBER?

Fin woke up.

A cold, black wind hit him in the face.

He was lying on a hard floor. And the floor was moving.

He tried to open his eyes. His head throbbed. Everything was blurry.

"Morning, sunshine," a voice said.

That's Roary, Fin thought. *Couldn't be, though, because she's safe back on the ship with Koal.*

"Welcome back to the program already in progress," another voice said wryly, a voice that unmistakably belonged to Koal.

Am I on the ship? Fin wondered. *Seems unlikely.*

Jesster's voice cut through his grogginess. "About time you re-joined the land of the living."

I thought they said they were taking us to the Cage, thought Fin blearily. *Not the ship.*

Look around, dummy. The cool, familiar thoughts of his sister flowed into Fin's head and even though his eyes still burned, they flew open.

Mo sat directly across from him. Kan stood next to her.

Chaaaaains, groaned Loathsome silently, curled up between them. Jellied black fluid oozed between the links of the thick chains holding the zombie horse prisoner. She kicked out her hind legs. The chains clanked.

And next to Loathsome was a very large purple box.

Thump-thump, thump, thump-thump went the box.

I hate you, Grumpo thought from inside it. *This is all your fault. I want to bite you so bad.*

"Grumpo!" Fin yelled. "I missed you so much!"

I didn't miss you at all because I hate you.

"WHO'S A GOOD BOY?" Fin asked in the voice you use to call a cuddly dog.

It is not me. I am a bad boy. Also not a boy.

"I hope you're not too mad," Fin said.

Grumpo thumped his box. *I don't judge. I hate you no matter what. I would hate you just the same even if you turned out to be a human with a pumpkin on your head. Oh. Wait.*

Fin laughed a little. "This is pretty messed up, huh?" he said to all of them.

Everyone was there, and everyone was clearly going to stay there for a while. Mo, Kan, Loathsome, Jess, Roary, and Koal stood against the silver bars of a massive cage hanging in the air a couple of hundred feet above the ground. Each had one arm locked to a bar of the cage and one foot locked to the floor. The cell swayed in the wind. Darkness waited below them.

"What's going on?" Fin said.

"Well, you've been out to lunch for ages," Koal chuckled. "The rest of us have been catching up."

Fin turned to his sister. "You came back!" He wished he'd said something cleverer, but his brain was having a rough go of it. "Where's Jax?"

"That's all you have to say?" Mo laughed. "I don't know, probably stroking his hunting trophies. Kan brought me back." The green-eyed enderman gave her a stern look. She'd promised. Mo rolled her eyes a little. "Kan rescued me. We teleported back to the ship and it was crawling with army boys yelling about Kraj and vengeance. So it sounds like you kept yourself pretty busy while I was gone."

"We've been sentenced to death by ender dragon." Roary sighed. "Good work, everyone."

Fin looked a little more closely. He peered through the bars to what lay outside the Cage. Obsidian pillars. Crystal flames. Silver cages. The ender dragon's island. Wonderful.

"Wait. Where is it? ED doesn't like to wait."

"It's flown by a few times," Mo said.

Flaaaaaaame, croaked Loathsome.

Mo patted her stiff, dirt-caked mane. *Yes, yes, you're very smart.*

"They're gonna hold a big ritual so everyone can see that Kraj was right and the human menace is real," Jesster explained. "Murrum is feeling pretty cut up about the whole thing now that his boss is toast and unavailable to yell at him or smack him around, so he wants to make sure everyone knows what a saint the old guy was. Spoiler," she said to Koal and Roary, who didn't know Kraj from any other enderman, "he was not a saint."

"None of you seem very worried."

ED would not hurt me, Kan thought. *I am an enderman. I have not done anything. You all are in big trouble, though.*

Why don't you just teleport away, Kan? Mo thought miserably. *Leave us. Save yourself.*

If I could take you all with me, I would. But I ran away too many times. I did not learn enough at the Enderdome. I am not strong or fast enough to take you all. So I will not leave. He took Mo's hand, and she smiled. *You are my End. You cannot leave your End.*

Fin was pretty sure Mo didn't think ED would burn her either. He was also pretty sure she was wrong. Fin had never liked the old beast as much as Mo did. It made him uneasy.

"These things tend to work themselves out one way or another." Roary shrugged.

"That's a very Chaotic thing to say," Mo observed. "You should come to church with us sometime."

Fin groaned and rubbed his head. It felt like he'd stuck it in a torch and let it slowly roast there.

"Never mind your head," Mo said eagerly. "We've been waiting for you to wake up."

"Why?"

Roary pointed at Fin's feet with a suggestive bounce of her eyebrows. Fin looked down.

He still had the grindstone.

"Wow! I can't believe they didn't take it off me!" He reached down with his unchained hand to make sure it wasn't damaged. "But it's no good without the books."

Koal smiled the smile of someone with a really good surprise ready and waiting. "We're way ahead of you, kid."

Mo reached out for him across the cage. He reached too. They couldn't touch. "Do you know what today is, Fin? So much has happened I forgot."

Fin shook his head.

"Happy Endermas, Fin," she said sweetly.

Oh. Oh wow. He just . . . hadn't realized. It had been the furthest thing from Fin's mind.

"They got us presents," Mo grinned.

Roary and Koal dug deep in their pockets for a minute. Then, Roary pulled out a book and tossed it onto the floor of the cage. It slid and spun over the wood and landed against Fin's big toe. The human girl reached in again and pulled out another one. And another. Koal already had five or six out. He pushed them toward Mo. Not all the books they'd had on the ship. But a lot of them. A respectable selection.

"Happy Weird Mysterious Murder Monster Day, guys," Koal said.

Fin picked up the book in his hand. He turned it over a couple of times. He and Mo locked eyes. They hadn't had a chance to talk about this. But they didn't need telepathy to sort out what to do next. It was now or never.

"Come on!" Roary coaxed. "I'm dying here!"

Koal crossed his arms. "This is going to be such a huge bummer if that's just a janky Bane of Arthropods spell."

"You first," Mo said.

Jess showed Fin how to use the grindstone. The book didn't seem to respond for a minute. Then it quivered. It swelled up like it meant to heave out a huge belch. It shimmered.

And it popped open.

All five humans, one enderman, one zombie, and one shulker leaned forward.

"Luck of the Sea Enchantment Level One," Fin read slowly. "The Luck of the Sea enchantment increases your chances of catching treasure rather than junk or fish. No *way*," he said in disgust and disbelief.

"I told you!" crowed Koal. Roary kicked him. "Sorry, though, Fin. Sorry."

Ha ha, Grumpo laughed in his box. *It is funny when you fail.*

Fin slumped down against the cage bars. "I can't believe it. I really thought . . . I really thought we would find something in there. Some answers. Anything." He threw the book onto the floor of their cage. "I'm gonna die and the only thing I know now that I didn't know before we went and royally screwed everything up in Telos is that you can add the Luck of the Sea enchantment to any fishing rod."

"Fin," Mo said softly.

"I'm really sorry, Mo. It all happened so fast. I didn't mean to kill Kraj. You don't know what he was planning, though. It's probably not the worst thing for the End that he's gone . . ."

"Fin," Mo said again.

"But I know that doesn't make it any better. I didn't kill him because of what he was planning. I just killed him because he hurt Jess and I hated him for it."

"Fin! Look!"

Mo pointed at the book. The stupid, useless Luck of the Sea Enchantment Level One book.

There was handwriting on the other side of the enchantment instructions.

Fin's handwriting.

As if in a trance, he picked up the book. At long last, Fin was front and center, reading to the class. He followed the words with his fingers.

It is always night in the End. There is no sunrise. There is no sunset. There are no clocks ticking away.

But that does not mean there is no such thing as time. Or light. Ring after ring of pale yellow islands glow in the darkness, floating in the endless night. Violet trees and violet towers twist up out of the earth and into the blank sky. Trees full of fruit, towers full of rooms. White crystal rods stand like candles at the corners of the tower roofs and balconies, shining through the shadows. Sprawling, ancient, quiet cities full of these towers glitter all along the archipelago, purple and yellow like everything else in this place. Beside them float great ships with tall masts. Below them yawns a black and bottomless void.

It is a beautiful place. And it is not empty.

"What is this?" Fin asked his twin.
"I don't know. Keep reading."

We have always lived here. We cannot remember any other place. We grew up here. It is our home. No different from any of the hundreds of endermen you'd find on any island here in the archipelago. We live on an end ship crammed with junk we snatched up from anywhere we could find it.

Fin flipped through the pages.

Kan's eyes aren't like the wide, clear magenta-violet eyes of other endermen.
Kan's eyes are green.

No one knows why. No one can remember any other enderman who had green eyes, not in all the history of the End.

"What in the name of the Great Chaos?" Fin whispered. He'd gone pale. He flipped faster through the book.

I'm going to call her Loathsome. Isn't that a nice name for a nice horse who definitely will not eat my brains the minute I'm not looking?

Mo trembled all over. "Skip to the end," she said, clutching her horse so tightly even the dead skin bruised.

Fin turned to the back of the book. He read aloud.

I am afraid. So much has happened. Kraj is dead by my own hand. Eresha is dead. I have lost my twin. The ender dragon is dead. Poor Loathsome. Poor Grumpo. Poor all of us. The End itself is coming apart. The islands cannot hold. The sky is falling. If I try to forget what I'm looking at, it's beautiful. Really. So beautiful. The towers of Telos are falling like confetti. It is coming. The great tide of memory will wash over me and I will know nothing about all this grief. And do you know? I think I welcome it.

I have retreated to the ship. Lying on the deck, I can watch the night tear itself apart. When I close my eyes, I can hear Kan playing somewhere far away. Good. He is alive. I'm glad. He's coming to find me. To be part of my End.

It's almost here. I can feel it moving through the
islands. Completely inevitable. Why fight it?

All hail the Great Chaos. Blessed be the Beginners.

See you on the other side, Ultimo.

Fin flung the book away from him in terror and bewilderment.
It skittered across the wood floorboards, through the bars of the
Cage, and soared out into the empty night. It looked like a white
bird as it plummeted away from them.

"What is that? What *is* it?" he cried, panicked.

"Okay, okay, calm down. Let's try another one," Roary sug-
gested. "Magic is always weird. There's an element of unpredictability in any enchanted object."

Roary disenchanted another book with the grindstone and
started to pass it round to Fin, then thought better of it and handed
it to Mo.

"The Feather Falling enchantment reduces damage from falling and damage from ender pearl teleportations," Mo read.

Then she turned over the page.

"This is my handwriting," Mo told them quietly.

She began to read from the other side.

It is always night in the End. There is no sunrise.
There is no sunset. There are no clocks ticking away.

But that does not mean there is no such thing as
time. Or light. Ring after ring of pale yellow islands
glow in the darkness, floating in the endless night. Violet trees and violet towers twist up out of the earth and
into the blank sky. Trees full of fruit, towers full of
rooms. White crystal rods stand like candles at the cor-

ners of the tower roofs and balconies, shining through the shadows. Sprawling, ancient, quiet cities full of these towers glitter all along the archipelago, purple and yellow like everything else in this place. Beside them float great ships with tall masts. Below them yawns a black and bottomless void.

It is a beautiful place. And it is not empty.

"I don't understand," Fin said, rubbing his cheeks. Nothing seemed real. What was this, what *could* it be?

Mo skipped to the end.

I am afraid. So much has happened. Kraj is dead by my own hand. Eresha is dead. I have lost my twin. But I believe he is alive. The ender dragon is dead. Poor Loathsome. Poor Grumpo. Poor all of us. The End itself is coming apart. The islands cannot hold. The sky is falling. If I try to forget what I'm looking at, it's beautiful. Really. So beautiful. The towers of Telos are falling like confetti. It is coming. The great tide of memory will wash over me and I will know nothing about all this grief. And do you know? I think I welcome it.

I have retreated to the ship. Lying on the deck, I can watch the night tear itself apart. When I close my eyes, I can hear Kan playing somewhere far away. Good. He is alive. I'm glad. The music is getting closer now. He's coming to find me. To be part of my End.

It's almost here. I can feel it moving through the islands. Completely inevitable. Why fight it?

All hail the Great Chaos. Blessed be the Beginners. See you on the other side, El Fin.

Roary disenchanted another. And another. And another. Koal had already stepped back. He wanted no part of it. It was all way too serious. An explorer has to expect a bit of getting sentenced to death by dragon. It was all part of the adventure. But this was too out there.

They took turns looking through the books and reading out loud. But it didn't matter. Each one was the same, in either Fin or Mo's steady handwriting.

It is always night in the End. There is no sunrise. There is no sunset.

It is always night in the End. There is no sunrise. There is no sunset.

It is always night in the End. There is no sunrise. There is no sunset.

See you on the other side, El Fin.

See you on the other side, Ultimo.

They weren't entirely identical. Some names changed. Some events didn't pan out the same way in every book. They didn't have time to really read them all. Soon they were numb to it. They checked the beginning and the end and moved on to the next disenchanted enchantment. It was all there. Their whole lives. Everything they'd ever experienced and a few things they hadn't yet. Over and over and over again in their own handwriting. And how many more of these had they left in the ship in that massive mountain of books?

Mumma, explaaain, thought Loathsome raspily, nuzzling Mo's hand.

I can't. I can't. I don't know.

Kan ran his hands over the books.

I'm in there, he thought. *In all of them. I'm playing my music as the world ends. That's something, I suppose.*

Fin strained for his sister. "Who is Ultimo?" he whispered to her.

"I have no idea," she answered. "Who's El Fin?"

"I don't know!" Fin spluttered.

Mo quirked her mouth to one side. She didn't want to say in front of everyone. But she didn't have a choice. "The ender dragon called me Ultimo," she confessed.

"Uh . . ." interrupted Koal. "Wait a minute. Go back. Ultimo? *The* Ultimo? Supreme Brewmaster Ultimo?"

"El Fin the Archmage?" said Roary, and her eyebrows said she was impressed.

I hate them, Grumpo huffed in his box. *They sound like losers.*

Jesster shook her head. "No way." She laughed. "We all like playing pretend, but no way. Ultimo and El Fin are *legends. Magicians'* magicians. Iconic. And they weren't twins. They're also dead. Presumed dead, anyway. Might as well be talking about King Arthur and Dracula. And like, no offense, but I saw you in action in the armory, Fin. I like you a lot. But you're not exactly iconic."

Fin tried to ignore that. He'd done his best, hadn't he?

"Saved you, didn't I?" he mumbled.

"Yeah, I saved you, too, my friend. Don't get it mixed up. This is not and never will be a damsel situation."

Fin couldn't help himself. In the midst of all that confusion and strangeness, he smiled a little.

Mo raised her hand from Loathsome's boil-covered back and set it back down again thoughtfully.

"What does it mean?" she asked no one and everyone.

But there was no answer to that, at least not one you could find in a cage hanging in the dark.

There was a commotion down below. A lot of grunting voices and soft thuds. Everyone lurched to one side of the cage to see what was going on down there.

A figure was standing on the sandy earth with its hands on its hips, looking up at them with intense irritation from inside a circle of severely wounded endermen.

"Oh my god, you freaking *dorks*," Jax shouted.

CHAPTER TWENTY

UNKNOWN VARIABLES

"Why'd you run off?" Jax called up to Mo from the ground. He sounded genuinely hurt.

"You were so mad at me. And you were gonna experiment on me."

"To help you!"

"I don't need help!" Mo shouted.

Jax laughed. "Cool story, you just hanging out in cages for fun, then?"

"We're going to be executed, *obviously*," Koal rolled his eyes. "Keep up."

"Dingus over here killed their president or whatever so now it's this whole *thing*," Roary jabbed her thumb over her shoulder at Fin.

"How can you be so casual about this?" Mo said. "They're going to kill us. You're acting like it's a joke."

Jess shrugged. "Nah. Jax is here now. We'll just escape. It's cool. We do it all the time."

"The ender dragon is out there somewhere, you know that, right? It won't just let us go."

"It's what I came for!" Jax yelled up. "One in the chest, one in the gut, two between the eyes and we're out of here."

"I'm not going to let that happen," Mo said quietly. Her voice was dead iron.

Koal's head snapped up. He looked out through the bars of the cage nervously. "Do you hear that?"

The ender dragon's island lay mostly empty. Even of the ender dragon. If the old lizard was here, it was hiding very well. Not like it at all, Mo thought. Jax had made quick work of the gang of enderguards below. The group was, for all they could tell, alone.

But then Mo could hear it, too. Then Roary. Then Jess. Then Fin. Then Kan and Loathsome and Grumpo.

Voices. Voices in the void.

Voices singing Endermas carols in unison, so loud that everyone could hear.

> O come ye, Great Chaos,
> Lawless and triumphant,
> Come ye, O come ye to the End.
> Come and reward us,
> Born your loyal fragments.
> O come let us obey you,
> O come let us assist you,
> O come let us adore you,
> Great Chaos above.

"Shoot us down already, would you?" hissed Jess.

Jax gave a very dramatic sigh. The human boy unholstered the crossbow on his back, took aim, and before Fin and Mo could scream that it was too far to fall, shot out the rope that held the Cage to the obsidian pillar.

They tumbled through empty space. Five kids, an enderman, a zombie horse, and a monster in a box.

Jesster, Roary, and Koal seemed completely unconcerned. Koal even waved at Fin in midair. Roary turned over on her back and made swimming motions with her arms. Jess checked her watch as they fell.

They had their elytra and Feather Falling boots. No fall could do much to them other than jazz up their funny bones. Fin and Mo used to have those things, too. But not anymore. They shot down through the sky with nothing to slow them down.

> O sing out, Great Chaos,
> Sing of pure anarchy.
> O come, O come ye to the End.
> Come and exalt us,
> Bring ruin to our enemies.
> O come, thou holy entropy,
> O come, thou blessed discord,
> O come, unknown variables,
> Chaos is born!

Grumpo hit the ground first. The lid of his box shot open, exposing the shulker to the air. He shrieked in rage and humiliation. Loathsome landed next. Her spine broke in half and her skull split open. But she was already dead, so it didn't really bother her.

Mo had always thought dying would happen fast. So fast you wouldn't know what hit you. But now that she was about to die, it all went so slow. A crawl, really. She had so much time while she plummeted toward certain doom. Time enough to see endermen flowing in toward the island from all sides, still singing their carols.

> O come let us embrace you,
> O come let us nourish you,
> O come let us delight you,
> Chaos is nigh.

Time enough to reach up toward Fin tumbling after her. Reaching for her hand, not catching it, reaching again. To see his blue eyes accept their fate. Time enough to see Kan, so far from her, teleport to safety without them. What else could he do?

Time enough to look up at the quickly retreating pillar where the Cage hung and see the ender dragon hanging upside-down below it like a vast and horrible bat. Its enormous black wings hugged its body. Its tail tucked up beneath those leathery curtains closed over ED's glowing face and ultraviolet belly. With its wings shut, you could hardly see it in the dark. Jax certainly didn't see it. He was standing right in front of it and he had no idea. If he had, he'd never have turned his back on it like that.

ED had been there all along. Waiting. Listening. An inch away from their feet.

As Mo fell, Jax began shooting out the crystal flames at the tops of the pillars. It was starting. The End. Whatever the End was going to be. This was it. One, two, three, the lights went out.

The last thing Mo saw before she hit the ground was Jax taking aim at the last lantern. Behind him, the ender dragon slowly opened its colossal reptilian wings.

Mo landed on Grumpo's box. Fin landed on top of her. They felt something horrid crack beneath them. Then, it seemed to sag and go soft and they were falling again.

The lid of Grumpo's box slammed shut over them. Thump-thump, thump, thump-thump.

> O come, thou holy entropy,
> O come, thou blessed discord,
> O come, unknown variables,
> Chaos is here!

The twins woke in an enormous purple chamber. The ceiling towered above them. The floor stretched out in all directions. Row after row of elegant columns connected the two. Torches lined the walls. Soft, golden light greeted them.

In the middle of the room they saw a raised platform made of the same purple stone as Grumpo's box. But it couldn't be. Grumpo's box was tiny. Stairs led up to a squat, square cube that looked very much indeed like Grumpo's box. And on top of that, angrily, resentfully, perched a naked shulker with nothing to protect it. A nub of pale, glowing, yellowish-green flesh. Not much bigger than a softball. Not much tougher than a gob of spit.

"Are you okay?" Mo asked gingerly.

"Is this your *box*?" Fin marveled.

Grumpo seethed on his podium.

"This isn't a shulker's box," Mo said. "I know shulkers. This isn't right."

"It makes a certain sense, you carrots, since I am not a shulker,"

Grumpo said. "Anyone with half a brain would have figured that out by now."

Grumpo *said*.

Grumpo talked. Out loud. Like a human.

Up above, outside the box, they could hear a riot of sounds. Furious sounds. The sounds of fighting.

"What are you then?" asked Fin. His throat was dry and thick.

The little softball-sized glob of slime rolled his eyes.

Grumpo bowed humbly. "I am the Great Chaos. Ugh, I hate the two of you so much. I really, *really* want to bite you."

CHAPTER TWENTY-ONE

ALL HAIL THE GREAT CHAOS

"Sorry, you're the what?" Mo said.

"You heard me, Ultimo. You always hear me. I am so tired of having this conversation. I have had it every way it can be had. It was fun at first, but once a thing becomes predictable, I become allergic to it, and the pair of you are giving me hives."

"You're the Great Chaos. The god of the endermen." Fin shook his head. "No, you're not. You're Grumpo! You hate everything and you yell at me and sometimes I give you an apple or a bit of cod for a treat at the end of the day."

"You can stuff your cod," the shulker growled. "I hate it."

Fin smiled. "There's my boy. WHO'S A GOOD BOY?"

"I am neither good nor bad and I am not your boy!" The shulker thundered. "God is a limiting word. I existed when the universe was new. I will exist when it burns itself out. I knew the Beginners, the builders of the End. I saw them come ashore, and do their work, and embrace their extinction. I am the eternal unpredictable stroke of chance in the cogs of creation."

Mo scratched the back of her hand. "What about the ender dragon? It talks like that. It said it was the infinite lightning nightlizard at the end of the universe."

"The ender dragon is my *dog*," Grumpo scoffed. "I got lonely a millennium or two ago. I needed someone to snuggle and amuse me with its tricks. Everyone needs someone to snuggle, you know. The development of a self-aware soul was a very good trick. As was fire breath. I am proud of ED."

"If you're so great and powerful, why do you look like a lump of snot?"

"—like a shulker," Mo quickly added at the same time.

"To observe you in this cycle and many others. The sight of my true form would liquefy your livers in an instant. Also everyone leaves me alone and I don't have to listen to those stupid carols. Once you're a god it's bye-bye to privacy. Paparazzi everywhere."

Fin said, "To observe us? Why?"

"Because I hate you," the Great Chaos grinned. "I hate you with such passionate intensity I cannot let you out of my sight. You really cannot imagine how much I hate you."

Mo sat down heavily on the floor. "Why is any of this happening? Why did you call me Ultimo? I don't understand."

"Aw, precious," Grumpo said kindly. "You don't understand because you're thick as a cake. That goes for the both of you. But don't feel bad. That's partly my fault. My dog ate your homework."

"Jax is gonna kill your dog if we don't get back out there," Mo pointed out.

"And why would I want to stop him? Someone always kills the ender dragon. It is the beginning of the cycle."

Mo felt as though she almost had it. She could feel the corner of it in her teeth but she couldn't get it out. The cycle. The enchanted books. The dragon's egg. Ultimo. All the pieces were there. But she couldn't make them fit.

"Chaos abhors a cycle," Fin said. He didn't know where that came from. It just popped into his head.

"*There* he is. There's the Fin I know. Of course, it's not entirely true. Scripture is like that sometimes. It sounds very clever, but the truth is so much more complicated. The cycle has never troubled me. I exist within the cycle. I set the cycle in motion. It's you two that broke it."

"How? What have we done?" Mo asked.

"You're stuck," said Grumpo. His voice sounded thick and wet. "And you cannot get out." The shulker's face, as much as a shulker had a face, grew serious. There was something almost like pity in his grey, milky eyes. "Oh, I have tried to help you. I told you not to let Kan on board. I told you to kill the humans. I told you you would be happier if you let me bite them. I even told Kan he could stay with me forever, because that would have been something *different*. Something chaotic. But you never listen. Not until it is too late. There will come a moment, after it is done but before it all begins again, when you will remember everything. You will know it all. What has come before a thousand times. What will come again. And you will cry your eyes out because you are human and that's what you do. I don't say that to mock you. It's nice that you can still cry. Gods cannot."

"Grumpo, please."

"I am not Grumpo."

"But you are," Fin insisted. "Part of you is. You can't live with us for so long and guard us from intruders and eat our popcorn without being a little bit ours. Our good boy."

The Great Chaos sighed. He squelched resentfully on the purple stone. Then, he spoke.

"I have said all this before and I will say it again. I hate you, Fin. I hate you, Mo. I hate you more than the last time I told you I hated you," Grumpo began. "The ender dragon is the heart of this world. It beats in the center of the End, round and round in circles, steady as a pulse. Nothing works without ED. And since the beginning, humans have come questing after it. To find ED and kill it for no particular good reason other than that it is kill-able. Every time my poor doggo dies, another one must be born. *That* cycle was perfectly acceptable. A world must have a heart. The ender dragon vanishes, an egg appears in its place, and a new ender dragon rises. But something as powerful and ancient and loyal to the Great Chaos who is its master does not die without leaving . . . a wake. Let's call it that. When a ship passes by at great speed, the sea churns and ripples after it as water is displaced and replaced again. That is what happens when the ender dragon dies. What is going to happen in about . . . oh, I would wager ten to fifteen minutes, give or take. A great wake pulses out from its body. It travels through the End like the tide. It touches every-thing and everyone. And it makes them forget. The world resets. What came before is gone. There is only the now."

"Why? How can that be good for anyone?" asked Mo.

"Why does your body respawn when you die?" Grumpo shrugged as well as he could without shoulders. "It is how ED decomposes. You shouldn't judge. You always were very judgey, Ultimo. It's a nasty habit."

"I am not Ultimo!" snapped Mo in frustration. "I'm just Mo! Just a girl with a ship and a horse and a twin."

The shulker laughed throatily. "Of course you're Ultimo. Ultimo the Magnificent. Supreme Brewmaster Ultimo. Do you think zombie horses listen to everyone? Sort yourself out, child. And you, you are El Fin the Archmage, the Flame in the Night. You were famous back home. Everyone wanted to learn from you. Ultimo lived in a vast graveyard with every kind of plant and mineral at her beck and call—people always get buried with their best loot. They used to say Ultimo could brew a potion to do anything under the sun or moon. Impossible things. Things no one else would even think of. El Fin lived in the desert, in a palace made entirely of torches. You met by chance, as far as I can tell. The two of you geniuses came down to the End for your turn at killing my dog many cycles ago. And you did it, didn't you? Bang—right between the eyes. But you just had to gloat. You didn't hop through your exit portal with your prize like most people. You stayed for *ages* and got caught in my poor puppy's wave of amnesia because you were just too proud of yourselves to practice basic personal safety. Disgusting. And so you go. Over and over.

"Some cycles are short. Some long. But they all end the same way. When you wake up, your pumpkins keep the Endermen from seeing who you really are, and of course you don't remember. The death of the ender dragon washes your mind so clean you can actually hear the thoughts of the endermen. Human minds are usually too noisy for that. And so you make certain assumptions. Humans are so good at making patterns out of nothing. Order out of . . . well, me. You patch over anything that doesn't fit. You *make* it fit. You look around at a ship and presume it's your home. You meet your neighbors and all of you are far too embarrassed to admit you don't remember one another so you invent reasons why you're feeling so out of sorts that morning. You do not need to stack, like the other endermen, to retain your mind, and you assume you must simply be . . . special. Not that you were never one of them. You see a shulker in a box and assume he's your pet. You have no parents, so there must be a story that explains why they're gone. And what archmage obsessed with fire does not hate the rain? Even when you would not know your own face in the mirror, some part of you remembered that. And then? You meet a strange boy who seems to like you, and imagine that you have been friends all your life. Mortal imaginations are astonishing. It's never more than a day before the End forgets that it's forgotten anything at all."

Mo looked inside herself. Was it true? Was it real? Was she Ultimo the Magnificent? But there was nothing. She couldn't remember any of it.

"What about Kan?" she asked. "He's not like us. He's not human."

Grumpo shut his eyes. "Ah, Kan. My enderman. My best enderman. I am the Great Chaos. The unknown variable is the gift I bring to the world. Kan is simply . . . Kan. He was born different. Those green eyes. A mutation. Mutations are the most valuable things in the universe. Without mutation, nothing ever changes. Because he was different, he did not belong. Because he did not belong, he sought out strangers when they came, hoping they would love him as his own people refused to. Don't get excited—you treated him no better than anyone else. Not during that first cycle. When the ender dragon's wave caught you, he was hiding nearby, trying to work up the nerve to talk to the beautiful brewmaster. And when you woke up . . ."

"He was there, so we thought we were connected," Fin filled it in.

"Yes. But that is the miracle of mutation. By imagining that you were connected, you *became* connected. Where there is Fin and Mo there is always Kan, now. And he has spent so much time with you, his thoughts embedded into the very brains of a pair of powerful humans, that he has developed beyond any other enderman I have ever known. The cycle has been messing with all my endermen. Each one of them bends and breaks and warps a little more with each version of this tiresome story. Or else they would never have thought to make Kraj a commander or organize an army or even make poor Eresha into the Mouth of the Great Chaos. Before all this started, none of them would have even dreamed of such fancy things! And frankly, it's terrible. Have you met Kraj? Ugh. He's *such* a bore. But Kan has changed the most. He's nearly human himself these days. And that music. That music. He is my proof. He is my justification. Kan's song is the illustration of all I am. From chaos comes beauty. You three became an End in yourselves. No one could have predicted it."

"How many cycles have there been?" Mo felt numb.

"This will be the thousandth cycle," answered the god of the endermen.

Fin and Mo gave up. They sprawled out on the floor and just lay there, unhappy and overwhelmed. Gravity was too much to bear just then.

"Why not just *tell* us?"

"What fun would that be? I told you. I tried to help. I tried to tell you. I tried to make each cycle different. But you are so stubborn! Humans love Order. They can't get enough of it. And you insist on being yourselves over and over."

"Wait . . . are we twins? Grumpo, is Mo my twin?"

The shulker chortled. "As I understand things, which is quite deeply, you met two weeks before you passed through your gate into the End. You are near strangers to each other. Isn't that just *fabulous*?"

"We have to break the cycle," Fin said finally. "That's all there is to it. We get out. And then we won't be stuck and everything will be normal forever."

The god of Chaos laughed.

"You always say that, Archmage. I have heard it nine hundred and ninety-nine times."

Mo didn't laugh. Mo frowned. She thought about Loathsome and Kan. She thought about Jess and Jax and Roary and Koal. She thought about Kraj and Eresha and Karshen and the note block echoing in the rainy night of the Overworld. It was all her End. If their shulker wasn't lying, they must have lived down here much longer than they ever lived up there. And until a few days ago, they'd been so happy.

"There," Grumpo crooned. "There's your trouble, Fin. She *likes* it here."

Fin ignored that. "You say this has all happened before. I read the books. I know you are at least telling part of the truth. But what about them? The humans fighting ED up there? Jess? Have they been part of the cycle before?"

Grumpo seemed surprised, almost. Taken aback. "No," he said thoughtfully. "They are new."

"So there's a chance," Fin leapt up. "There's a chance we can change things. We can break the cycle and escape. We'll take Kan with us, Mo, if that's what you're worried about. We'll take him and we'll start a new life. Build a house. Till a field. Together."

Mo looked so uncertain. "If we're together, everything will be okay. That's how the universe works. Weren't you listening?"

Fin grinned at Mo. The old playful grin she'd known all her life. All her life that mattered.

"Ooh, I can't wait to see how this turns out," Grumpo snarked. "What suspense."

Something crashed down on top of the box. Dust trickled down through the stones.

"You'd better hurry," Grumpo said as if it didn't matter at all to him. The pair got up to go. They climbed the platform stairs toward the lid of the box.

"Please, my children," the Great Chaos called to them in a suddenly soft, gentle voice. "Remember, no matter what happens, no matter what you do or say, no matter if you live or die, no matter if you achieve your dreams or drink their ashes, I will always, always hate you. Until the end of time, I will hate you more than anything in the cosmos."

Fin frowned. A strange idea came into his head. "Grumpo, when you say you hate us, do you really mean you love us? Is this a Great Chaos thing? Are words meaning the same thing as the dictionary says they mean too much Order for you? It's a pretty terrible joke, you know."

"You wish," snorted the shulker. He nodded behind him. "Please exit through the gift shop," he joked to himself. Neither Fin nor Mo laughed. They didn't know what a gift shop was.

The sound of the door closing echoed through the Great Chaos's lair.

"See you back on the ship," he said to the shadows.

CHAPTER TWENTY-TWO

THE FINAL BATTLE, AGAIN

Ultimo the Magnificent and El Fin the Archmage exploded out of the shulker's box. They landed on a battlefield already burning.

The enderman holiday choir hid behind pillars or simply fled. The ender dragon roared in injured fury. It dodged and flew between the pillars, bleeding freely from one wing. Jess and Koal were encamped in the center of the island on the stone courtyard, weapons drawn, waiting for ED to drop low enough to end it all. Roary ran between them, doling out healing potions. Jax whooped and hollered. He danced in the scorched earth. He reloaded his crossbow for the killshot.

"No!" cried Mo. She leapt at him and knocked the arrow out of his hand.

"You *melon*," he snarled. "What are you doing?"

"I'll explain later!"

Jax rolled his eyes and shrugged her off. It was time for battle and he had no interest in listening to her innermost thoughts.

The ender dragon saw them. Its white eyes blazed. It folded its wings and dove straight for them.

"Yeah! Let's go! This is it!" Jax laughed with delight. "Final checks, everyone! Got your coats? Got the keys? Anybody need to go to the bathroom? No? Then let's DO THIS!" He notched another arrow and put the dragon in his sights. He fired.

ED opened its monstrous purple jaws. It ate the arrow like it was nothing.

Then it ate Jax.

It happened right in front of Mo. One minute he was there, dancing from foot to foot, trash-talking an ancient deity's favorite pet. The next minute he was gone. A lonely bow fell from the sky.

"Oh my god," gasped Fin. "Oh my *god.*"

"ED, stop!" screamed Mo. "It's me! It's me!"

But ED was the infinite lightning night-lizard at the end of the universe and it didn't care. ED was doing what it was made to do. Protect the End from outsiders. Nothing else mattered. And Mo was an outsider, too. She'd never been anything but.

The ender dragon turned on her. With a shriek it swooped down to devour her as well. Mo took off at a dead run. But it wasn't just ED. Everyone was shrieking. Everyone was screaming. Everything burned around them.

Kan? Mo thought wildly. Where was Kan? Where had he teleported to? Was he safe? Fin shoved her down just as ED pulled up, catching his upper arm with one claw. El Fin the Archmage cried out in pain.

Mo ate sand. *This. This is the Great Chaos. Death and battle. It seems like a game until everything's on fire and your friend is dead.*

Roary tossed her a healing potion from behind a pillar. The dim light of the End caught the glass bottle. It sparkled briefly— and then ED barreled through again. The bottle shattered. A rain of healing misted down, too diffuse to help anyone.

Especially Roary. Lying face down on the rock. Her eyes closed.

Fin screamed wordlessly. *No, no, no!* They knew now! They were supposed to be fixing the cycle! Everything was supposed to be okay!

"Help!" yelled Koal over the din. "Fin, Mo! Help!"

They scrambled over the broken stones through the storm of flame and debris toward Jess and Koal. A pair of endermen had them pinned down, punching at them with bare fists.

"Karshen," breathed Mo.

It was Kan's secondary hubunit. And Koneka, the fragment Fin had met outside the Enderdome. The fragment from Kraj's brainbank squad. Two wasn't quite enough to achieve enlighten- ment. It was just enough to be *really* good at fighting and know why you wanted someone dead.

Fin searched the ground—a sword. Someone's, anyone's. No. Not anyone's. His. Theirs. Their treasure. Borrowed by an ender- man and left where it lay. Mo was already crawling toward a tri- dent.

She was closer than he was. Fin waved to Mo.

Go, go, go! Go without me! I'll be fine!

Karshen hit Koal over and over. Koneka went at Jess with bare teeth. Fin got his hand around the fallen sword. Mo rolled over with the trident clutched in her blistered fingers.

But it didn't matter. Not much does when there's a dragon in- volved. ED sped through the air toward the little grey courtyard. Fin's legs pumped under him, willing the distance between him and Jess to disappear. Jess, who just wanted to build her library and live here in the End like they had. Jess, who saved him. Jess, who he saved. Jess, with her long brown hair and her constantly rolling eyes. Fin sobbed. He hadn't even gotten a chance to tell her how glad he'd been that she wanted to stay.

Mo almost made it to them. She would have made it. But unknown variables will have their way.

Loathsome rocketed out of nowhere. Her bloodshot eyes streamed tears. The undead demon horse collided with her mother, knocking her out of the courtyard. The mare turned round to look at Mo just as ED opened his mouth and emptied his gullet onto Jess, Koal, Karshen, Koneka, and Loathsome, engulfing them all with white-hot fire. The humans went to ash in an instant. Fin didn't even have time to call Jess's name. Koal's face went slack with total disbelief, then drifted away like dust. Till the last second, he simply knew he was going to escape. He always escaped. Karshen dissolved into smoke. Koneka looked up at the infinite blackness of the End. *It is lonely out here on the dunes,* Fin heard her think, and then she was gone, too.

Loathsome burned. Her undead body was the candle. Her long mane was the wick. She burned and burned. Mo sobbed. She held her arms out to the horse, but she couldn't touch her. The flames were too hot and fierce.

Mumma! Loathsome cried out in her mind. *Slain. Slaaaaain.* The dead horse stumbled to her knees.

Why, Loathsome? Mo's thoughts were soaked in tears. *Why didn't you stay safe like we told you, you beautiful dummy?* She stretched her arms out to the creature she could never touch again. *Don't die. Only dummies die.*

Mo reached out into Loathsome's gentle ghoulish soul for the last time. She saw the infinite graveyard. The wiry trees. The sickly moon. The gravestones, all written over with new things. EATING FLOWERS. RUNNING IN THE RAIN. MUSIC. CAGE IN THE SKY. MUMMA. DRAGON! MUMMA. ULTIMO THE MAGNIFICENT.

And one read: GOODBYE. A rotting, moldering hand scrabbled up out of the grave dirt.

I love you, Mo thought to the graveyard of her baby's mind.

The hand waved sadly. Then it went still.

Fin and Mo stood in the middle of the carnage, slack-jawed. They'd never had a chance. How could anything happen that fast? It wasn't fair. You couldn't fix it. If it wasn't fixable, it shouldn't be allowed to happen that fast.

Through his tears, El Fin the Archmage whispered, "We can still break the cycle. If we find Kan. He can teleport three of us back to the Overworld. That's not too much. ED's still alive. If we leave now, it can't start over again."

But Mo couldn't move. She couldn't leave Loathsome. She couldn't even leave Jax, flying around up there in the belly of the ender dragon. *Three days ago I was happy*, she thought, and lay down on the earth with her hands over her head. What did it matter what happened? She wasn't Ultimo the Magnificent. She didn't even have a brother. She was nothing.

The song didn't have time to start out quiet. It burst into the air at full volume, rich and lovely and sad and sweet and complicated, like everything else. Mo knew that song. She turned her head, looking for the source.

Fin tried to see through the smoke and his own tears. He knew that song, too. *But Kan shouldn't be here. He should stay safe. Stay away. Grumpo told us. Kan never stays away.* Ash settled onto his hand. Fin stared at it and shuddered. He dropped below the smoke layer and crawled to where Jax had dropped his crossbow. He wrapped his arms around it and held it tight. ED wasn't going to get Kan too. It just wasn't.

But ED wasn't going after Kan. It wasn't moving.

It was *listening*.

The ender dragon cocked its head to one side, listening intently to the music. Its muscles held perfectly still. Kan advanced out of the shadows, playing his note block better than any note block had ever been played or ever will. His green eyes glowed in the black fog.

Mo put her hand on Fin's arm. He nearly jumped out of his skin.

You scared the life out of me! he thought wildly.

Mo looked deep into his eyes. Eyes that had been purple until three days ago. She held him tight. And between their minds they understood everything in an instant. They didn't have to plan. They didn't have to argue.

Kan can't die, thought Mo. *No matter what it costs.* And a moment after that: *And none of the rest of them, either. It's not their fault their vacation turned into our nightmare. They don't deserve to lose everything.*

I don't want to remember anyway, Fin thought. *We failed. I don't want to remember we failed.*

The End is what counts. Our End.

They were both holding the crossbow.

Fin let go.

Mo stood up and strode across the island. The End burned behind her. Her hair glowed in the light. ED turned to see her. It heard no more music. It saw no other prey. Only her. The ender dragon spread its black wings into the sky, bellowed to the heavens, bent down, and launched itself toward her. Mo didn't flinch. She aimed and she fired true.

Game over, the ender dragon bellowed into her brain. *Try again?*

The bolt took the ender dragon between the eyes. The lights went out in ED.

But not before the colossal bulk of its body slammed into Ultimo the Magnificent, crushing her mercilessly against the stony earth.

Ash, smoke, embers floated through the air. Kan and Fin ran to her, never once thinking they could make one bit of difference.

They found two things where Mo died.

Her body, and a glistening black-and-violet egg.

CHAPTER TWENTY-THREE

A TIDE OF MEMORY

Fin alone sat on the deck of the ship. The night flowed all around him. There was a certain taste in the air. A tang of ozone and burnt obsidian. Telos crumbled in the distance. The End was coming apart. Getting ready to be reborn. Only this time without her. And no one would know the difference.

He remembered everything. El Fin the Archmage. His life in the Overworld. What pigs looked like. How many times he had discovered how big Grumpo's box really was. Everything. In that magical space between the End and the Beginning, his mind was completely clear.

But he didn't much care.

He held a book in his lap. One of the ones from the hold. The empty hold. At the end of the last cycle it'd been crammed full to bursting. No war that time. No Commander Kraj. This time he'd have to start from scratch. In every way. The book was *Curse of*

Binding Level Two. Fin turned to the first page. *You can add the Curse of Binding enchantment to any piece of armor such as helmets, chestplates, leggings, or boots . . .* it read.

El Fin the Archmage turned the page over and began to write on the back.

> I am not afraid anymore. So much has happened. Kraj is dead by my own hand. Eresha is dead. Karshen and Koneka are dead. Mo is gone. The ender dragon is dead. Poor Loathsome. Poor Grumpo. Poor all of us. The End itself is coming apart. The islands cannot hold. The sky is falling. If I try to forget what I'm looking at, it's beautiful. Really. So beautiful. The towers of Telos are falling like confetti. It is coming. The great tide of memory will wash over me and I will know nothing about all this grief. And do you know? I think I welcome it.
>
> I have retreated to the ship. Lying on the deck, I can watch the night tear itself apart. When I close my eyes, I can hear Kan playing somewhere far away. Good. He is alive. I'm glad. He's coming to find me. To be part of my End.
>
> It's almost here. I can feel it moving through the islands. Completely inevitable. Why fight it?
>
> All hail the Great Chaos. Blessed be the Beginners.
> See you on the other side, Ultimo.

A cool hand slipped into his.

"Not if I see you first," Mo said.

Fin went pale. Then he tackled her in one of the greatest and fiercest hugs in recorded human history. "You're alive!"

One of the Telosian pagodas tumbled off the side of the island into the void.

Mo patted her pocket.

"Totem of Undying. Brings you back feeling like roadkill. But it brings you back. I understand how to use it now. So here I am. You can't keep a good brewmaster down."

They lay back on the deck of their home, looking up at the starless night. The starless future. They listened to Kan's music, getting closer and closer as he walked toward them. Not teleporting, but walking, as his friends did. As his End did. He would be here soon. He quite literally couldn't be late.

"I wish we'd fixed it, like you wanted," Ultimo said. "I think I've said that exactly a thousand times."

"I don't know," Fin sighed. "Maybe we're as fixed as we're going to get. It's only . . . them. Jess and Jax and Roary and Koal. They didn't deserve to get mixed up in our little dance down here. They should be up there. Kicking pigs and dancing in the rain."

Mo brushed her long, dark hair out of her face.

"About that," she said. "I don't think Ultimo the Magnificent can really take an L that big. It's just not in her nature. But . . . you know what that means."

Fin nodded.

"Can you make that choice for them?"

El Fin the Archmage squeezed her hand. He stroked her face with his hand. Not his twin. But still his family.

"You saw them. The cycle is getting worse. It's evolving. It's changing the laws of nature. Endermen use weapons and build armies and . . . apparently humans don't respawn. I'm only here because of my totem, and here's hoping I remember to grab another one on the next go-round. They should have woken up in their own beds. But you saw them. They were just lying there on the ground.

Cold and quiet and *gone*. We can't leave them like that. We just can't. And you never know. Grumpo said they were new. Maybe this is what changes everything. Maybe this time it's different."

Mo nodded. She pulled a few things out of her infinitely deep pockets, assembling them on the deck with the practiced ease of an expert. Five potions in a neat row. Regeneration potions, but more powerful than any the Overworld had seen since Ultimo the Magnificent lit out for parts unknown.

"If it's not," she said as she finished, "that's okay, too. I've had a good thousand lives with you, Fin. A thousand more won't hurt."

"But will they remember us? If this works? If they come back like we do? Will we remember them?"

Mo sat back on her heels. "No." She sighed. "I don't think we will."

"I don't want to forget again. I don't want to forget Jess. Or any of them," he added quickly.

"Me neither. But we never remember." She capped off the potions. "At first. Maybe this time there will be some small thing that's different. That sparks us. Like it did this time. Maybe it'll be Grumpo or Loathsome or ED or something Kan says or the glint in Roary's eye. Maybe it'll even be awful old Kraj. Maybe it'll be Jax calling me a melon or Koal laughing or Jess swinging her sword. Maybe all of us together . . . maybe we'll *stack*, even though we're humans. Become something more than we were separately. Something. Something new. Something . . . Chaotic. And maybe we'll begin to remember next time. Before it's too late. When there's still time for remembering to matter. Maybe this time, we do it all right. And everything changes."

Kan's dark head appeared over the side of the ship as he floated toward them. He let his note block fall silent. They didn't have to say anything. They never did.

Fin, Mo, and Kan walked down into the hold together and sat down to rest. Then, Mo decided nothing could really be awkward when the universe was collapsing. She snuggled into Kan's side. Fin leaned against their backs. And they waited. The slumber party at the end of the world.

"Can you feel it? I can feel it coming," she whispered. "Like a tsunami. First the water retreats, and for a minute you think everything is going to be okay. Then it rises up and washes everything away. I love you."

"I love you too, Ultimo," Kan said. He squeezed her tight. "You really were magnificent."

Mo winked. "You too, green. You too."

"See you on the other side," whispered El Fin the Archmage.

The wave of memory passed over the ship an hour later. Fin and Mo and Kan fell asleep long before it came. The world shifted, and tilted, and righted itself, and remembered nothing.

About an hour after that, the shulker box at the back of the ship creaked open. Something emerged. Not a shulker. Not an enderman. Not a creeper or a skeleton or a witch or a human. Something the color of a shulker, and the shape of the unpredictability of all life.

Very gently and tenderly, Grumpo fitted a pumpkin onto Fin's head, and then Mo's. He'd do the same for the others when they turned up. It wouldn't be long now. Grumpo tucked in the vines and made sure they looked nice and neat. He bent down and kissed each of their foreheads.

"I hate you both so terribly much," the Great Chaos whispered. And vanished.

The atoms of the player were scattered in the grass, in the rivers, in the air, in the ground. A woman gathered the atoms; she drank and ate and inhaled; and the woman assembled the player, in her body.

And the player awoke, from the warm, dark world of its mother's body, into the long dream.

And the player was a new story, never told before, written in letters of DNA. And the player was a new program, never run before, generated by a sourcecode a billion years old. And the player was a new human, never alive before, made from nothing but milk and love.

You are the player. The story. The program. The human. Made from nothing but milk and love . . .

Shush.

Sometimes the player created a small, private world that was soft and warm and simple.

Sometimes.

—Julian Gough, Minecraft "End Poem"

CHAPTER TWENTY-FOUR

THE END

It is always night in the End. There is no sunrise. There is no sunset. There are no clocks ticking away.

But that does not mean there is no such thing as time. Or light. Ring after ring of pale yellow islands glow in the darkness, floating in the endless night. Violet trees and violet towers twist up out of the earth and into the blank sky. Trees full of fruit, towers full of rooms. White crystal rods stand like candles at the corners of the tower roofs and balconies, shining through the shadows. Sprawling, ancient, quiet cities full of these towers glitter all along the archipelago, purple and yellow like everything else in this place. Beside them float great ships with tall masts. Below them yawns a black and bottomless void.

It is a beautiful place. And it is not empty.

The islands are full of endermen, their long, slender black limbs moving over little yellow hills and little yellow valleys.

Their narrow purple-and-pink eyes flash. Their thin black arms swing to the rhythm of a soft, whispering music, plotting their plots and scheming their schemes in the tall, twisted buildings older than even the idea of a clock. They watch everything. They say nothing.

Shulkers hide in boxes nestled in ships and towers. Little yellow-green slugs hiding from outsiders. Sometimes they peek out. But they snap their boxes safely shut again, like clams in their shells. The gentle thudding sound of their cubes opening and closing is the heartbeat of the End.

And on the central and largest island, enormous obsidian towers surround a small pillar of grey stone ringed with torches. A brilliant lantern gleams from the top of each tower. A flame in a silver cage, shooting beams of light down from the towers into the grass, across a little grey courtyard, and out into the black sky.

Above it all, something slowly circles. Something huge. Something with wings. Something that never tires. Round and round it goes, and its purple eyes glow like furious fire.

Fin!

The word came zinging through the shade off the shore of one of the outer islands. A huge end city loomed over most of the land: Telos. Telos sprouted out of the island highlands like something alive. Great pagodas and pavilions everywhere. White shimmers fell from the glistening end rods. Shulkers clapped in their little boxes. Leashed to Telos like a dog floated a grand purple ship. A pirate ship without an ocean to sail. Most of the end cities had ships attached to them. No one was certain why, any more than they're certain who built all those big, strange cities in the first place. Not the endermen, though they were happy to name every place after themselves. Not the thing flying in endless circles around a gate to nowhere. Not the shulkers who never came out of hiding long enough to learn anything about anything. The end ships just *were*, as the cities just *were*, as the End just *was*, like clouds or diamonds or Tuesdays.

Fin! Find anything good?

A skinny young enderman teleported quickly across the island, in and out of the nooks and crannies of Telos. He blinked off in one place and back on in another until he stood on the deck of the end ship, holding something in his arms. His head was handsome, black and square. His eyes were bright and hungry. His limbs were slim but strong. An enderman leaned against the mast, waiting for him. She crossed her dark arms across her thin chest.

Nothing good, Mo. Just a bunch of pearls. We've got tons of those. Ugh. You take them. They give me the creeps. I was sure the chestplates we found last week would regen by now but I guess somebody else got there first. I got some redstone ore. That's about it. You go next time. You always sniff out the good stuff.

The twin twelve-year-old endermen, brother and sister, Fin and Mo, headed down into the guts of their ship. They'd always lived here. Here on the ship with their two brothers and their two sisters. Jax and Koal and Jess and Roary. And every day, their dear friend Kan would visit. Kan was tall and dark and thin like all the enderfrags were. Taller than Roary but shorter than Jax. He had big, beautiful eyes, but he was always squinting, trying to hide them, trying to make them unnoticeable.

Because Kan's eyes weren't like the wide, clear magenta-violet eyes of other endermen.

Kan's eyes were green.

And he played the note block better than you'd ever believe a note block could be played.

Jax liked to tease Mo that she was sweet on Kan. Brothers were like that.

They couldn't remember any other place.

They grew up here. It was their home. No different from any of the hundreds of endermen you'd find on any island here in the archipelago. They lived on an end ship crammed with junk they'd snatched up from anywhere they could find it. Some of it was *very* good junk. Diamonds and emeralds, gold ore and lapis lazuli. Enchanted iron leggings, pickaxes of every kind, beetroot seeds and chorus fruits, saddles and horse armor (though they'd never seen a horse). Dozens of sets of marvelous grey wings you could stick right on your back and fly around anywhere you liked. Some of it was just plain old actual junk. Rocks and clay and sand and old books with broken spines. A moldy greenish-blue egg with weird veins running all over it. Fin and Mo didn't care how ugly it looked. They put the egg by the fire and hoped for something unpredictable to happen. Something new.

The family of endermen knew there were other worlds out there. It was only logical, when you lived in a place called the End. If there was an End, there had to be a Beginning. Somewhere else for this place to be the End *of*. Somewhere the opposite of here. Green and bright, with blue skies and blue water, full of sheep and pigs and bees and squid. They'd heard the stories. But this was *their* world. They were safe here, the seven of them, with their own things and their own kind and their own story.

One big happy End.

ABOUT THE AUTHOR

CATHERYNNE M. VALENTE is the *New York Times* best-selling author of dozens of works of science fiction and fantasy, including *Space Opera*, *The Refrigerator Monologues*, and the Fairyland series. She has won or been nominated for every award in her field. She lives on an island off the coast of Maine with her partner, her son, and several other mischievous beasts.